Other Schiffer Craft Books on Related Subjects:

Framing Floral Techniques: Floral Design Skill Building, Inspirations & Explorations, Renee Tucci AIFD PFCI, ISBN 978-0-7643-6200-2
The AIFD Guide to Floral Design: Terms, Techniques, and Traditions, American Institute of Floral Designers, ISBN 978-0-7643-6425-9
Styling Beyond Instagram: Take Your Prop Styling Skills from the Square to the Street, Robin Zachary, ISBN 978-0-7643-6318-4

English-language edition © 2025 by Schiffer Publishing, Ltd.

Originally published as *Design Floral*, © Éditions Eyrolles 2023, Paris
Translated from the French by Lisa Tripp

Library of Congress Control Number: 2024941499

All rights reserved. No part of this work may be reproduced or used in any form or by any means—graphic, electronic, or mechanical, including photocopying or information storage and retrieval systems—without written permission from the publisher.

The scanning, uploading, and distribution of this book or any part thereof via the Internet or any other means without the permission of the publisher is illegal and punishable by law. Please purchase only authorized editions and do not participate in or encourage the electronic piracy of copyrighted materials.

"Schiffer Craft" and the crane logo are registered trademarks of Schiffer Publishing, Ltd.

All photos © Guillaume Langlais, except for the following.
© Blømeko: pages 32, 35. © Clément Bouteille: 25. © Collectif de la Fleur Française: 18 top. © Domestika: 4. © Émilie Eychenne: 145, 147, 148. © Iconographia: 134. © Justine Beaussart: 6, 11 left, 12 center, 13 top left, 13 bottom left, 18 bottom, 57 top left, 57 top center, 62, 63, 64 (with spiral: Freepik/brgfx), 73 (montage with Shutterstock photos: 73 left: BestPhotoPlus; 73 top left: Maurese; 73 top right: FewDimoib; 73 bottom: Aldina Abaza; 73 right: Oleksandr Kavun), 76, 82, 123, 138, 140, 141, 142, 143 bottom. © Laurence Revol: 149. © Shutterstock: 11 center: smspsy; 11 right: Jacqui Martin; 12 left: Mala Iryna; 12 right: OLAYOLA; 13 top center: Iva Vagnerova; 13 top right: aleksandrastachura; 13 bottom center: Gina Hsu; 13 bottom right: IanRedding; 19: ricardo.araujo330; 27: Emily Geraghty; 57 top right: David Charlton; 57 bottom left: Kwanbenz; 57 bottom center: Miguel Toro; 57 bottom right: NEKOMURA; 58 top left: Victoria Kurylo; 58 top center: sergey23; 58 top right: pilialoha; 58 bottom: images72; 59 top left: zcebeci; 59 top right: Max_555; 59 bottom left: Trubaieva Svitlana; 59 bottom center: Julitt; 59 bottom right: Hatice Sever; 61 top left: Sahara Frost; 61 top right: Petersham Plantsman; 61 bottom left: freya-photographer; 61 bottom center: Negrobov; 61 bottom right: Shutter Chiller; 65: Sandy Storm. © Martin Condomines: 129 top. © Ulrike Pien: 22. © Wikimedia: 139 left: DcoetzeeBot; 139 right: Jane023. © Établissement Studio: 120, 121.

Cover design by Lori Malkin Ehrlich
Interior design by Julie Simoens
Type set in Bodoni 72 / Assistant Light

ISBN: 978-0-7643-6939-1
ePub: 978-1-5073-0567-6
Printed in China

10 9 8 7 6 5 4 3 2 1

Published by Schiffer Craft
An imprint of Schiffer Publishing, Ltd.
4880 Lower Valley Road
Atglen, PA 19310
Phone: (610) 593-1777; Fax: (610) 593-2002
Email: Info@schifferbooks.com
Web: www.schifferbooks.com

For our complete selection of fine books on this and related subjects, please visit our website at www.schifferbooks.com. You may also write for a free catalog.

Schiffer Publishing's titles are available at special discounts for bulk purchases for sales promotions or premiums. Special editions, including personalized covers, corporate imprints, and excerpts, can be created in large quantities for special needs. For more information, contact the publisher.

We are always looking for people to write books on new and related subjects. If you have an idea for a book, please contact us at proposals@schifferbooks.com.

ACKNOWLEDGMENTS

This book was made possible thanks to a combination of small and large acts of kindness, as well as by shows of support and trust from numerous people dear to my heart, whom I must thank. First, thank you to all the passionate floral designers who have generously passed on their knowledge to me, and from whom I've had the good fortune to learn my profession: Massimo Pilastro, Davide Bandiera, Luigi di Gioia de Mada, Michela Pozzato de Fiori, Gaetano d'Abbene, and Samantha de Fiorinmente, along with the merry team at Pampa. Big thanks also go to all the professionals who agreed to contribute their words to this book: Hélène Taquet from the Collectif de la Fleur Française (French Flower Collective), Marlène Mazières of the Les Batisses flower farm, John Jastszebski of SODIF, Clément Bouteille of her eponymous flower farm, Cécile Bertin of Cili Brtn, Romain Chirat from Établissements Studio, Dorothée Lemaître of Solange Talents, Émilie Viala of Marwee, and Simoné Eusebio of Make My Lemonade. Thanks also to all the photographers who agreed to have their work appear in these pages: Guillaume Langlais, Émilie Eychenne, Martin Condomines, Iconographia, and Laurence Revol. And naturally, a very loving thank you to my entire family. To my grandparents, who filled my childhood with flowers, and to my parents, Nadine and Francis, Marcel and Murielle, for their support. Thank you to Danielle for proofreading, and to Remy for his precious advice. Thanks to my husband, Paul, for having watched our little Alda all alone through my long nights writing during the first few weeks of our new life as a family of three. Thank you to my best friend, Lisa, who encouraged me to switch to a creative profession, and with whom I have regularly collaborated since the creation of Nebbia Studio. I feel lucky and proud to be by your side in your wildest floral dreams. Thank you to everyone who follows @nebbiastudio on social media. You drive me to do more to share my adventures and you keep me engaged with spirited conversations. And lastly, thanks to Éditions Eyrolles for having offered me this magnificent opportunity.

FOREWORD

My name is Justine. I founded my floral design business, Nebbia Studio, in 2021.

Like many in my generation, this is my second career, and it's quite different from my first. After graduating with a degree in communications, I started out working in advertising agencies in Paris and Milan. In 2017 (also the year I turned thirty), I was spurred by the need "to do something with my hands." I began to work toward switching to a more creative and craft-based profession.

After three years of training, Nebbia Studio was born. In addition to the standard curriculum to earn my Florist Occupational Certification (*CAP Fleuriste*), I trained in other areas, reading various books, doing online research, attending workshops, and completing training programs with professional mentors in France and Italy.

Many aspects of my job resonate with me deeply: attention to detail in client relationships, the broad range of projects, and the creative approach to working with flowers. I get to choose unique varieties grown in environments that respect both nature and people, and can develop and experiment with eco-friendly floristry techniques.

I don't follow the typical florist paradigm. I create floral sets for advertising and fashion shoots, assist visual artists and ceramicists who need specific plants for their work, make floral backdrops for boutiques and restaurants, and design floral decor for private events like weddings.

This book focuses on topics I care deeply about, and presents a snapshot at a moment in time that summarizes what I've learned over these past five years. I'll show you the very personal way in which I work, and I encourage you to double down on your reading and experiences to further expand your own knowledge.

Working with plants has provided me with an abundant source of joy that completely shook up my world, shifted my habits, and stirred my creativity. I hope from the bottom of my heart that this book will encourage others to passionately embrace the handcrafted world of floral design!

CONTENTS

1. SOURCING FLOWERS — 9
Seasonal Flowers — 10
Flowers in Your Business Plan — 14
The Various Players in the Sale of Flowers to Florists — 19
The Strong Resurgence of Dried Flowers — 32

2. THE FLORAL DESIGNER'S TOOLBOX — 37
Tools for Cutting and Shaping — 41
Tools for Hanging, Fastening, and Gluing — 43
Tools for Watering and Maintaining Moisture — 45
Transport Materials — 49
Materials for Decorating and Wrapping Arrangements — 51
Items for Setting Up Your Studio — 53

3. THE BASIC PRINCIPLES OF FLORAL DESIGN — 55
Choosing Flowers — 56
Making a Successful Floral Arrangement — 62
Understanding Color Harmony — 64

4. THE MAIN STAGES OF A FLORAL DESIGN PROJECT — 69
Defining the Project — 70
Ordering and Prepping Flowers — 80

5. PUTTING ECO-FRIENDLY FLORAL DESIGN TECHNIQUES INTO PRACTICE — 85
Prepping Plants — 87
Types of Projects — 89
Packaging and Transport — 114

6. WORKING ON YOUR COMMUNICATION SKILLS — 117
Your Visual Identity — 119
Your Portfolio — 123
Your Website — 128
Social Media — 131

7. CASE STUDIES — 135
Dutch Still Life with Iconographia — 136
The Event at the Make My Lemonade Boutique — 141
Marie and Alex's Wedding with Atelier Jeanne Pons — 145

Conclusion — 149
Resources — 151

CHAPTER 1

SOURCING FLOWERS

Like a chef who is always on the lookout for a new flavor to elevate a recipe, I love to search for specific varieties of flowers. I'm looking for that unexpected element that will provide originality to the arrangement and make all the difference. To do this, I try to build relationships of trust and respect year after year with the people who provide me with the raw material essential to my work. Whether they're horticulturists or wholesalers, we all share the same love and respect for plants.

Sourcing flowers is one of a floral designer's main activities, and how they are sourced is essential. Indeed, the service you're offering the client depends as much on the quality of the plants you have chosen as on the beautiful creative product you'll provide. You need to be able to count on reliable suppliers who are transparent about their products, so that you can make thoughtful, well-informed decisions.

I personally have paid careful attention to this step since starting my business, while espousing the eco-friendly values that go along with it. I first consider the seasonality of the plants, because the practices that respect their natural rhythm will yield much-higher-quality flowers. These flowers are beautiful and strong and last longer in the vase. When you work with seasonal cut flowers, you'll experience a rollercoaster of emotions all year long. You're always having to leave behind your favorite varieties, only to then rediscover them later—it never gets old! Building on that approach, I try to source my flowers as locally as possible. This allows me to support my local horticultural industry, while limiting transport, which impacts both the quality of the flowers and the planet.

These were all reasons why I joined the Collectif de la Fleur Française when I established Nebbia Studio, committing to use a minimum of 50 percent nationally grown flowers over the course of a year. I strive to exceed that goal as much as possible, although there are still significant gaps when sourcing French flowers in our country. However, things are starting to stabilize, thanks to the commitment of various players, who we will discuss in this chapter.

While sourcing plants in an environmentally responsible way represents a challenge in and of itself, with constraints and compromises, it makes the resulting satisfaction all the greater.

Seasonal Flowers

WINTER

Come wintertime, you must learn to be patient and appreciate the beauty of certain local varieties, whether grown outdoors or in a greenhouse. Wherever you are in the world, as a flower designer you will have learned the seasonality of your local area, and you can decide how far your "local" distance limit is in terms of the winter varieties you choose. In my case, since my shop is in France, I primarily work with wholesalers who buy their flowers from the Var, a French region with a mild climate and a well-developed winter floriculture. This is also the time of year when I tend to source more flowers from Italy, a neighboring country with a similarly mild climate. Last, to top off my selection, where necessary and depending on the project, I look at what's available from the Netherlands. You can follow the same practice of looking nearby to determine your best sources.

My favorite flowers during the winter period are ranunculus. They first turn up at market stalls in early

November and continue until late April, or even early May in the case of some small flower farms. They come in a wide range of colors and I love to play with their palette. They also have the advantage of lasting more than a week in the vase if the water is changed regularly.

Anemones are also winter stars. Their lovely silky and delicate petals have the unique feature of closing when it's cold and opening when it gets warm.

Winter also gives pride of place to conifers, branches, pine cones, and dried fruit, which are used in colorful fashion to enliven Christmas wreaths and centerpieces for the end-of-year holidays.

Winter Flowers

Ranunculus, anemones, poppies, tulips, mimosa, freesia, narcissus, hellebores, wallflowers, snapdragons, birds of paradise, forsythia, amaryllis, broom plants

RANUNCULUS

ANEMONE

POPPY

SPRING

The appearance of the first spring bulbs in late March is like nature's alarm clock. 'Belle Epoque' tulips, crown imperial, 'Petit Four' narcissus . . . these pretty and poetic names gently rouse us from hibernation, as Mother Nature gradually awakens. This is also the season for flowered branches such as cherry tree or lilac, which lend a majestic feel to arrangements. And how could we forget the most awaited peony, which makes its debut in late April or early May, honoring us with its presence until June. Of all the spring flowers, it is certainly the most popular with my clientele.

During this season, my favorite flower of all is the bearded iris. It comes in countless captivating colors, with wavy petals so elegant they take your breath away.

IRIS

PEONY

SPIREA

Spring Flowers

Iris, fritillaria, tulips, sweet pea, campanula, phlox, roses, arums, freesia, bells-of-Ireland, foxtails, lupines, nigella, cherry blossoms, foxglove, lilacs, and peonies.

During this period, I particularly appreciate being able to work with small local growers, whose fields are overflowing with wonders. I love talking to them about their latest new offerings and how they are experimenting on future treasures.

SUMMER

Summer boasts a parade of blooms, each variety more incredible than the next: Portuguese squill, giant alliums, lisianthus, lilies, roses—the show is at its peak!

It's hard to choose my favorite flower, that's how much I cherish them all, from the delicate scabiosa to the robust gladiola. For me, summer is the season where everything is possible, every color and every texture. Dreaming up floral arrangements becomes a nearly limitless exercise.

Summer Flowers

Roses, helianthus, gladiola, statice, China aster, phlox, scabiosa, amaranth, campanula, lilies, allium, cosmos, African lily, celosia, hydrangea, lavender, sunflowers . . .

Sourcing Flowers

GLADIOLA

SCABIOSA

LILY

FALL

Although the available range of flowers slowly begins to dwindle, I'm still very fond of the fall period for its warm colors. Once the season has really taken hold, I wait impatiently for my favorite moment: those few short weeks when the last of the giant dahlias rub shoulders with the very first 'Vienna Copper' or 'Spider' mums. The combination of these two flowers yields arrangements that are equally rich in texture and volume.

Fall Flowers

Dahlias, Japanese anemones, asters, sedum, Aztec marigolds, chrysanthemums, zinnia, amaranth, nerines, ornamental cabbages . . .

DAHLIA

AUTUMN CHRYSANTHEMUM

JAPANESE ANEMONE

Dahlias happen to be my favorite flower of the season by far, even though they don't last very long in the vase. I grow certain varieties in the garden for my own use. I love to pick them, arrange them in a vase on the table in my dining room, and watch them evolve. I've even learned to appreciate their decline, petals shedding one by one, as much as their initial splendor. Fall is also the season of incongruous pairings, when vegetables rub shoulders with the flowers. Ornamental cabbages, and even those oddly shaped gourds, provide a fun final flourish to arrangements. The only limit is your imagination.

Flowers in Your Business Plan

When you venture out to your neighborhood florist, you get that pleasant feeling of getting closer to unspoiled, idyllic nature. You press your nose into that lovely spring-colored bouquet, thirsting for a scent that invokes the sweet memories of childhood. Fields, birds, butterflies, and fresh morning dew all come to mind.

Unfortunately, we now know that the reality of the flower industry is far from that storybook image. Faced with logistical, ecological, and economic problems, florists sometimes have a hard time aligning good values with market forces. As we perpetuate a very old craft, we need to challenge certain work habits. This does entail a certain degree of adaptability, but I believe it is our responsibility to take on these issues. We must develop a practice that is more respectful of the environment and informs our consumers. This will allow them to make well-guided decisions while getting the most out of a piece of nature that has not harmed the planet.

My experience in learning about these things for my business planning came from seeking out the details of my local floral-industry ecosystem. Your experience will be similar, as you learn the ins and outs of how your work with flowers fits into the context of your geographic area.

Although the details I'll share with you relate to my spot on the globe, I believe the information will be useful to you and applicable in many ways as you consider your own situation. For example, although the industry experts who helped me—and who kindly share their insights with you in this book—are the people I've learned from in France and in Italy, all of us in the world's floral community share many of the same general challenges and business goals, and we can learn from each other.

WHERE THINGS STAND

Currently, North America's cut flowers industry has a healthy outlook: estimates vary, but it's projected to grow steadily at least through 2030.

Its environmental impact right now is less positive. Most of the flowers arranged so beautifully have been grown quite far from North America and represent a significant environmental impact. Indeed, they are often cultivated in heated greenhouses to change the seasonality of the plant, or in hot-weather countries such as Kenya or Ecuador, where low-paid laborers work under conditions that are difficult to control.

Watered with phytosanitary products and later transported by plane, the plants are stored in energy-intensive cold chambers. As in many other industries, the cut-flower market is largely globalized. The nerve center for this industry is Aalsmeer in the Nether-

The Specific Nature of Flower Auctions

Whether it's the immense Aaslmeer in the Netherlands, the Los Angeles flower market, New York's flower district, Ontario's Mississauga flower market, or others, buying directly at a major floral market offers a dazzling variety. Many offer non-auction as well as auction sales.

Wholesale purchases of cut flowers are structured around the principle of reverse auctions, also called "clock auctions" or "Dutch auctions." This system, which was invented in 1870, allows suppliers and buyers to negotiate the rates of the plants in record time.

The "clock" refers to the large screens that stream photos and information about the plants for sale: property, origin, quality, and the available quantity. The auctions then take place in descending order: the highest rate is posted and then drops rapidly, cent by cent, until one of the buyers presses the button on their desk to stop the count. The first buyer to respond is the one that gets the lot at the last posted price. The difficulty is in choosing the right time to act: if you press too early, you risk paying too much, but if you wait too long, the lot could disappear from right under your nose!

---

lands. Flowers from all over the world pass through a 1,065,627 sq. ft. (98,999.99 m²) hangar daily, before they are by turns negotiated, purchased, and redistributed.

There are flower and foliage farms in every state of the US now, and in most provinces of Canada. In the United States, cut flowers and florist greens raised domestically were valued at nearly $763 million in 2022, according to the USDA's National Agricultural Statistics Service.

About 10,800 commercial farms grew those domestic flowers and greens that year, and that is an increase of over 50 percent from 2017. So there has been progress made.

Imported cut flowers to the United States, in comparison, were valued at $1.9 billion in 2022. With our business choices, we can move the industry in the right direction.

Take part in your state floral association, as well as your area's local guild. Many of the associations connect all the players, including florists, growers, and wholesalers. And all are focused on supporting the industry, and on educating you. Many have specific programs focused on local sourcing, ethical long-distance sourcing, and eco-friendly business practices. Your state's agricultural extension can offer you useful details as well.

As for consumers, those who are well informed no longer hesitate to ask sellers where their flowers come from, so that they can buy responsibly.

Interview with Hélène Taquet of the Collectif de la Fleur Française

To illustrate the amazing energy focused on local sourcing, I decided to give the floor to Hélène Taquet, who is the founder and president of the Collectif de la Fleur Française.

Can you tell us about the goal of the Collectif de la Fleur Française, of which you are president?

The Collectif's main goal is to publish an annual directory online for consumers that lists florists who use at least 50 percent French flowers during the year. This list is composed both of French wholesalers and growers.

The second goal is to connect French flower professionals so that they can work together toward the common good.

What notable developments have you been able to observe since the association was created in 2017?

The cut-flower industry was on its last legs. The Collectif provided a new impetus to make cut-flower production local again, around consumer centers. We now total more than 500 members who can inform, train, and share our experiences with consumers and anyone wanting to join these professions.

In your opinion, is government action needed to safeguard the cut-flower-production industry in France?

Action must first and foremost come from each one of us. That's how to make things happen. We know too well that everything the government does is overly complicated. An association like ours is free to act quickly and properly. This makes each member accountable and gives free rein to all initiatives. However, facilitating the flow of information between SAFER (Rural Settlement and Land-Use Development Agency) types of institutions, chambers of agriculture, horticulture and floristry schools, as well as unions, would clearly speed up the transition and restructuring of the cut-flower industry.

What concrete actions should florists implement?

First of all, florists are too often still yielding to ease of sourcing, without worrying about the origin of the flowers. Similar to the agreements made among major distribution players, it seems to be essential at this point for florists/wholesalers to engage with flower growers, to make local production sustainable and determine a long-term strategy.

Florists then have an informational role. Why do consumers only ask for roses? Because that's the only thing they know! Florists should provide information about the origin of the flowers, the different kinds and varieties. They should be excellent storytellers.

Your book *Dare to Farm Flowers* (*Oser la ferme florale*) is an informationally rich guide for people who want to get started as flower growers. In your opinion, what is currently the main obstacle to embarking on that path?

There are a number of obstacles to cultivating flower farms. I'll mention three of them, in order of importance.

1. Logistics.

2. Florist loyalty and commitment.

3. Land access and the difficulty of obtaining bank loans.

Collectif de la Fleur Française
www.collectifdelafleurfrancaise.com
@collectif_delafleurfrancaise

The Various Players in the Sale of Flowers to Florists

When it comes to sourcing flowers, I have a two-step process to find what's available on the market. First, I contact the flower farms in my region directly to consult their offerings, and then I supplement my selection from my wholesaler, who buys nationally and, when necessary, internationally. I therefore buy either directly from the person who grew the plants, or through a third-party intermediary, a wholesaler.

FLOWER PRODUCTION

Who produces flowers?

Cut-flower production is organized within small-, medium-, or large-sized concerns that grow and sell flowers. Their customers are primarily wholesalers and florists. We'll differentiate between two types of producers.

Medium and large producers grow significant quantities of flowers. Their flowers are sold to wholesalers, and national and international buyers, either through their own distribution means or via clock auction (see page 15). These flowers may also be sold directly to florists via wholesale trading centers, or through each producer's individual sales platforms.

A single person will often manage small flower farms, which are of limited size. They produce lower quantities but offer numerous, unusual varieties. They sell their production in a short distribution channel, primarily to florists but also directly to consumers in the markets. Note that some wholesalers have begun to offer the flower farms around their warehouses the opportunity to sell their flowers there. This is the case with SODIF—more about that on page 28.

I discovered the world of flower farms in 2017, while I was living in Milan and my career transformation plan was just beginning to take shape. The only knowledge of sales channels I had was what I had learned while preparing for the professional certificate program. In other words, I knew about the classic "wholesaler/florist" relationship.

My introduction to this world came from the SlowFlowers Italy association, which at the time had a handful of florists and small producers. Since its founding in 2017, SlowFlowers Italy has organized a festival in Tuscany each year to raise awareness among the public and flower industry professionals about the environmental stakes of cut-flower production.

Interview with Marlène Mazières of Les Batisses Flower Farm

To delve further into the topic of sourcing, I interviewed Marlène Mazières, who founded her flower farm in the Dordogne region of France.

Marlène, can you tell us a little about what you do?

I have cultivated cut flowers and foliage in the heart of the Périgord-Limousin Regional National Park since March 2021. I farm land owned by my parents, who were cattle ranchers. I've chosen to work in a larger area (just under 4.94 acres [2 hectares]) to take advantage of the different biotopes that are naturally present: full sun, wooded, and wetland. The surface area that is actually planted is smaller, since I'm the only one here for the time being, but it's gradually increasing with the seasons.

What was your career path before flowers?

I spent my childhood not far from my current farm, but I lived in Paris for twenty years when I attended university and worked as a set designer. I completed a dual degree in industrial design and engineering because I wanted to design planes; I used to dream about them. I got my diploma when the 2008 financial crisis hit, and, through the biggest coincidence, I found myself working in the luxury sector, in interior design/architecture initially, and then for different fashion houses. I was able to dive into what now brings me the greatest joy on the farm: colors, textures, shapes. That experience was in part my initiation to everything beautiful, and now I'm the one who's cultivating it.

How did you train to be a flower grower?

I didn't complete a classic curriculum; I did a remote training program with Floret Flower in the United States for six weeks in January 2020. Everything I currently do, I do with the help of different sources (online, books, mainly English-speaking authors) and my own intuition, because I'm starting to know my land, my climate, and the surrounding fauna better and better.

I've been lucky enough to have access to my parents' land to farm. Without that, I would not have been able to get started without any formal prior training.

How do you choose the flowers that you grow in your fields?

This is the part I like best, and I could spend hours on it (especially at night and in winter). I consult many sources, from new publications or old books (often in English) to horticultural magazines, websites, Instagram posts, etc. I write down my finds in notebooks, and I then try to learn as much as possible about them, whether it's seeds, cuttings, or young plants. I also use sticky notes to list all the plants present in the field. I choose perennials for their aesthetic qualities: interesting fruit in winter, pretty shades of leaves, flowering branches, flowers you rarely see at florists (such as irises—*Iris germanica, Iris sibirica,* or *Iris ensata*—which I'm particularly fond of).

For annuals, I try to offer different coordinating shades, so that my clients can make balanced arrangements, and so that I can experience the pure pleasure of walking among those rows each day. It's such a difficult profession; you need to create beauty for the eyes and the heart. Lastly, I also look at the trends, because as in my previous career (fashion), they influence demand.

How is your work organized over the year?

There's no real break, unless I decide to take one. Contrary to what you might think, you can be busy daily in winter. I seed throughout the year, which means those seeds need to be babied; I also have two "cold" (unheated) tunnels, which means I can plant starting in fall, so that things are ready come early spring. And in winter I watch over the plantings that are underway, protect them from the cold or wind, and clean the beds from the previous year, if that step wasn't already completed.

I also plan the entire next season by using spreadsheets, which serve as my guide during the season's rush. They also allow me to know what to seed and plant, and where in the field to do so.

From March to November, plantings are constant and my daily life is dedicated to maintenance, picking, and sending plants, because I ship 90 percent of my flowers all over France. I also tend to administrative tasks and customer relations, which are very important to me.

What is the biggest difficulty you had to face this year?

Juggling all the steps I previously mentioned while being alone on the farm. I'd like to find help for next year to try to get one free day for myself per week. It would allow me to think about how the location is being developed and the work being done there. The heat wave was also very hard; plants are resilient, but it's always difficult to see them suffer and feel powerless about it.

What has been your biggest joy?

All the new varieties I discovered! Notably chrysanthemums, whose great diversity is not well known in France, because here they are always associated with All Saint's Day. Similarly, the only varieties you can get are in pots, which are compact and come in strong colors. Another great pleasure was seeing the field take shape, the site come to life, and the animals (reptiles, birds, mammals, amphibians) cross paths and each play their role.

What are your plans for the upcoming seasons?

I'd like to start developing hybrids, creating new varieties. There are so many colors that are not easily found in Europe (outside the United Kingdom) that would be interesting to delve into. The plant world is so rich and complex—it's endless, it's a life's work! I would also like to share the field more. I've started to host three-day workshops this year in collaboration with one of my florist clients. The discussions with our participants (often professionals from the flower world) are very layered. It's also interesting to have both a flower cultivation program, and a training program on how to work with flowers, in a single location. This also allows us to review how flowers are grown and how to enhance the value of local, sound production. It demonstrates that we can make something beautiful without having to source products from far away.

www.les-batisses.com
@les_batisses

The first time I attended this festival, it was merely as a curious visitor. By the next year, I was a volunteer helping to organize it. On that occasion, I found flower producers who were passionate about working with the earth, concerned about respecting their soil, and concerned about maintaining biodiversity. They are resilient people, for whom flower production is both a life plan and an agroecological process.

The flower farm model has also been rapidly expanding in other places too, of course, including France, I'm pleased to say. As I am writing this in 2023, a new flower farm is established in France at the rate of one every four days.

The Difficulty with Sourcing

As a florist wanting to source from these small flower farms, my main hurdle is finding the right logistical system.

Some flower farms who sell to neither the wholesale trading centers nor wholesalers offer shipping by mail or delivery of pallets by freight carriers. Others set up collection points or local deliveries. Despite everything, I often need to comb the countryside around me to get what I want from growers in my area. While I personally am happy to do it for ethical and ecological reasons close to my heart, this might pose a significant obstacle for some of my colleagues. I therefore believe that logistics will be the biggest challenge for small flower farms in the upcoming years—in other words, finding solutions to facilitate the flower-sourcing process. That is something all members of the industry should be thinking about together.

The "Local Flowers" Initiative in Lyon

Noting the growing demand for local flowers at florists in his city, while also running into the logistical sourcing challenges I've addressed in this chapter, Romain, a committed designer from the floral boutiques Les Imparfaits in Lyon, France, decided to take matters into his own hands. Along with his team, in the spring of 2022, he launched the concept of "Local Flowers," a professionals-only market featuring flowers from small growers in the region. He rounded up the items in stock in his Les Imparfaits shop and presented them to florists in a WhatsApp group message. Group members could then instantly reserve whatever lots interested them and come pick them up at the point of sale. The "Local Flowers" initiative might someday allow Romain to make his dream come true, which is to launch his own little flower farm in the countryside.

Interview with Clément Bouteille

For another flower grower's point of view, I interviewed the founder of Clément Bouteille Fleurs, established in 2021.

Hello Clément, could you introduce yourself?

My name is Clément Bouteille. I'm a plant professional who wears many hats, with a business in the south of Lyon between the Monts du Lyonnais and Mont Pilat. After working for several years as an event florist, I moved back to my family's land in 2019 to create a flower farm; I now have a nursery as well. I grow cut flowers and potted perennials, in addition to working as a florist (using 99 percent of my own flowers) and gardener (which was my first career).

Why did you choose to grow flowers?

As a florist in Anvers, Belgium, and later in Paris, I had the opportunity to work with incredible flowers, little known and exceptional varieties, which for a certain time allowed me to meet my botanical needs. But the disconnect to the real world of plants and seasons drove me to launch my current project.

I've always been interested in plants and growing. I love every part of a plant; a branch, the fruit, or a root can be just as interesting as a flower. I'm happy to be able to share this passion for the entirety of the plant world with my florist clients.

What is your favorite variety to grow and why?

I don't have a favorite variety. I love so many things and my favorites change. But let's just say that all the ones I grow are kind of my favorites. Often, the ones I like most are not classic cut flowers. I'm thinking of my collection of botanical blackberries, which produce magnificent branches and foliage for my clients. I of course love botanical lilies, *Paphiopedilum*, although in our climate we tend to prefer *Cypripedium*. They also form my logo, so I have to grow them! I don't think I have found my favorite plant yet. That being said, there are varieties that I particularly love, because they are fertile, easy, and productive: 'Tokyo' chrysanthemums, dahlias, and amaranth, to name a few.

Can you tell us a little about how your distribution channels have evolved since you started your flower farm?

I don't have any definitive channels yet; I've tried almost everything, from the wholesale market, florists, private individuals, etc. Currently, all flowers are sold either directly to florists or through a wholesaler. That's the direction I want to maintain, and that best fits my aspirations.

What is the biggest difficulty you had to face when you opened your business?

I think I was very lucky, because I had family land, equipment that was already partially on-site... I did not have any tough moments when I was setting things up. We usually create our biggest difficulties ourselves.

The fact of starting small and slowly expanding, being willing to listen to the market, to clients, and to adapt my business to my situation all allowed me to avoid some of the difficulties I might have encountered.

And your biggest joy?

There is joy every day, or almost. Awaiting a new flower, or when there's a new seedling that grows even though it was failing until that point, a customer's surprise at a delivery, the passionate discussions between passionate people, life everywhere in the gardens, living with the rhythm of the seasons; it's magical.

What are your plans for the upcoming seasons?

I foresee two major challenges for my flower farm. The first is to create a stable clientele, so that collaborations are well established and ongoing. The second is finding a way for those clients, wholesalers, and florists to make a more definite commitment. The goal is to have clear visibility about their future purchases in the year, in order to then be able to safely schedule

investments to properly develop the farm (purchase of new bulbs, landscaping work, etc.).

Another plan for the upcoming year is to open my nursery of botanical perennials, primarily from Anatolia and eastern Europe, which will allow me to diversify as well as increase the number of varieties I grow and collect.

I also have certain plants that I am planning to start growing seriously; hellebores, to name but one.

www.clementbouteille.com
@clement.bouteille

WHOLESALERS

Wholesalers are essential players in the cut-flower industry. They buy flowers in bulk from the various global, national, and local markets, and then sell them to professionals.

Wholesalers manage all of the logistics inherent to transporting plants from the point of production or point of sale. They are an important ally with extensive market knowledge who can give you well-informed advice and find solutions to sourcing issues.

In order to have a smooth working relationship with your wholesaler, it is important that you really understand their operations. Determine which days the flowers arrive, delivery days, and order deadlines.

For very specific requests (a very large quantity of a single variety, a rare plant, a very specific color, etc.), start planning much earlier than your usual order date, so that your buyer has enough time to find what you need.

Sourcing Flowers

When it comes to sourcing flowers, each wholesaler has its preferences. SODIF (with which I work regularly) is a major wholesaler at the market in my region. It is very clear about its desire to support the local horticultural industry. It's a member of the Collectif de la Fleur Française (see page 16), and its aim is to become a national point of reference for this sector of the economy.

RUNGIS MARKET

Interview with John Jastszebski, executive director of SODIF

To get a more specific perspective on the world of wholesalers, I contacted John Jastszebski, executive director of the SODIF flower distribution company, a business that has thirteen warehouses in France and is committed to supporting the flower industry.

What made you decide to manage SODIF?

My older brother took over 100 percent of my parents' farmland. I didn't particularly want to continue in that business sector, so I sold him my shares. My goal was to then invest in taking over a company. I had been living in Paris for ten years at the time, and I was looking for a life change. As I worked with my parents on this project, we first became interested in two companies in Rungis, one that specialized in the sale of plants, and the other in decor. Those two projects never came to fruition, but we then found out that SODIF, which is headquartered in Mâcon, was being sold. I went to see it in June 2016, and things happened very quickly from there. The sale was finalized that October.

How did you train for your new profession? What steps did you take to move into this new business sector?

SODIF has been around for fifty years. It had two generations of managers from the same family. So I'm in some ways the third generation who is continuing to operate the business.

When I came in, the former directors stayed on to assist me for six months. I wanted to proceed in stages, in order to properly take over every aspect. The first year, I delegated the administrative portion, which allowed me to initially focus on understanding all the other areas. My plan was to take the time to get an overview of the company's business, by moving from position to position. I started with the so-called "distribution" jobs, in which flowers are received in the morning and then distributed. That was the best way to rapidly learn the names of the flowers and the differences between the varieties, to understand their specific features and see how they were packaged.

I then moved on to local purchase and delivery, which we call "mobile sales." There's a truck that travels, selling flowers directly to florists. It's a sales method that requires you to know your customer perfectly. Since there's not a lot of storage space in the truck, you have to choose with exact precision the flowers you bring. I then moved from job to job, from procurement supervisor to procurement secretary; that's a position that is directly linked to product sourcing. After that stage, I decided to set out on a pilgrimage to figure out "how things grow." Initially, I specifically visited growers in the South of France.

Can you describe the different types of sales at SODIF for us? What options are available to me as a florist?

Let's start with the most common purchasing method available to florists: online. The florist logs on to the wholesaler's online platform and accesses all the available information about the products: price, origin, size, and color. As a general rule, an order placed that morning will be delivered the next day. Note that these purchases are made on the Dutch market, so there will not be any flowers coming directly from local French producers, or in any case, those flowers would have passed through the Netherlands for logistical reasons.

At SODIF, online sales through an online store represent less than 15 percent of florists' purchases; we are well below the national average. We still do a lot of preorders "manually," through direct contact or over the phone.

We also have mobile sales, which I spoke about previously, with trucks that go directly to flower shops. At SODIF, we go two to three times per week. With each run, the truck will have a slightly different assortment of stock, because the flowers in our warehouses come in from different places almost every day of the week: deliveries from the South of France generally come in on Tuesdays and Thursdays, the Paris region delivers on Wednesdays at the height of the season, and of course flowers come in from the Netherlands almost every day, as do any imported flowers. The logistical time can vary depending on the sector. Additionally, there's a third purchasing possibility, cash and carry, which refers to on-site sales at our warehouses. This is ultimately where we have the widest range in volume, since it includes locally grown flowers from the South, and the Paris region, as well as flowers from the Netherlands, Ecuador, etc. You have everything right in front of you in the same place. Regardless of the purchasing method, I think it's important to say that a relationship with a wholesaler is built over time, season after season, as the flowers become available on the market. Once the relationship is solid, it's automatic. You need to be patient and be a good communicator.

Could you explain to us how SODIF purchases from growers in France? How does that relationship work?

For us as wholesalers, we have two options. We can buy in clock auctions or buy directly from growers. In France, clock auctions are operated by SICA, the flower market in Hyères. They have a lot of flowers grown in the Var region, as well as flowers that come in from Italy.

As far as direct purchases from growers are concerned, we work with several production areas in the country. Know that the majority of flowers grown in France are exported. For example, I'd say that 60 percent of French peonies are exported.

If you only serve clients on the French market, you have to try to find areas and growers that are less exposed to export demands, that take different approaches, and that are not located just in the Paris region. We also list many small flower farms that are located around each warehouse. Some truck farmers also grow flowers at a given time of year, to produce a single product.

These are truly relationships that come from creating a network, with the aim of enhancing the region's value. From the moment we made it clear that we wanted to focus on French flowers, more and more growers have heard about us and contacted us. We also organize meet-ups for florists and growers at our warehouses.

Could you tell us how SODIF's desire to showcase French flowers came to be? What actions are you taking and what objectives still need to be met?

Before COVID, French flowers were a one-man battle for me. I had tried a little, but I was not very successful with either my clients or my teams.

In February or March 2019, I met Audrey and Mathilde of Désirée, who told me about the Collectif de la Fleur Française, and I saw the possibility for a larger-scale initiative. Then COVID hit and everything sped up. To make a long story short, I had wanted to collaborate with growers from the Paris region for a long time, and I had begun contacting some of them. But at the time, they didn't see much benefit to working with me. They were already used to selling at Rungis [a wholesale trading center; it's also the largest fresh produce market in the world], and that was just how it was. Then, during the first lockdown, there was the whole "lily of the valley for our elders" initiative with the Collectif de la Fleur Française. We organized deliveries of French-grown lily of the valley to hospitals.

After that, some growers, who no longer had any way of selling all their flowers at the Rungis market, started sending us their flowers. That allowed us to keep working during the lockdown, using almost exclusively all French flowers.

Many phone numbers were exchanged at that point! Once the market resumed, some of them went back to their old practices, but we maintained our sales relationships with other growers. We even established production contracts with some of them, such as Valentin Brossard's family for lisianthus, lily of the valley, and sweet pea. This allows growers to know how much product they'll be able to sell to us during their season. We do the same thing with small flower farms that are just starting out. They may have a clientele of reliable florists they sometimes sell to directly, because they got their start together (a grower who is just beginning will be more likely to offer their flowers to nearby florists than to wholesalers, thinking that the latter is interested only in volume). This network allows them to get started, but with the knowledge that, should they produce more in the future, we can take on the rest of their production.

As concerns our goals for developing the French flower market, some people say that the main problem goes back to supply, and that there are not enough growers on our territory. I understand the argument, especially in terms of the available range, but I do think some nuance is warranted. Every week, we offer French flowers in our warehouses, but sadly, every week much of that stock remains unsold.

SODIF tends to get three specific types of florists:

- "Old-guard" florists, who buy exactly the same thing every week. They are very reliable.

- The "in-betweens," who have their doubts. They would like to offer different ranges or other varieties, but their clientele does not always respond favorably.

- The new generation of florists. They are very open minded and very demanding about the current issues we have noted. They come to SODIF because we work with flowers from the Paris region, or because we are starting to have a small network of local producers. Conversely, they are inconsistent with their flower sourcing. One week they are there, but then not the next... It's very hard to gain their loyalty, which makes it hard for us to predict demand.

More generally, in terms of the goals to be met, I think that if we can be better organized at the industry level, there is still a lot of potential. Also, our collaborators' clients are still evolving and developing new ideas, which I'm quite sure will lead to more commonsense solutions.

www.sodif-fleurs.com
@sodiffleurs

The Strong Resurgence of Dried Flowers

Fashion is an eternal cycle: what was outdated yesterday can become trendy once again in an instant. And dried flowers are a textbook case!

Over the past few years, they can be found everywhere and in every form: in bouquets, wreaths, glass cloches, and bridal accessories. They are sold at floral designers as well as at major home decor retailers. They come in natural, bold, or faded shades.

Personally, I don't really love working with dried flowers, but I understand why consumers are drawn to them (they're natural and long lasting), and why florists benefit from being able to manage stock with a nonperishable raw material.

In France, cut dried flower production exists, but cannot meet the current considerable demand. At the European level, there are imports from the Netherlands, Italy, and Germany. Many flowers also arrive from much farther away, notably China.

Numerous wholesalers offer wide varieties of dried flowers and strive to diversify and freshen up their supplies in a variety of colors.

As for flower farms, in most cases they offer local varieties that have not been treated or dyed.

Environmentally Unfriendly Dye

The ecological side of dried flowers reaches its limits when the plant has been dyed or faded, because unnatural products are needed in both cases. It's an important factor to consider when you want to make well-informed purchases or choose between different products.

Interview with Clara Meurisse, founder of Blømeko

To learn more about the subject, I turned to Clara Meurisse, a florist who specializes in dried flowers. In 2021, she founded Blømeko, a sustainable dried-flower boutique.

Clara, can you introduce us to your business?

After several years as an engineer in the industrial world, I decided to change to a profession that is more in sync with nature. At the time, I was attending floral-arts classes, which helped give me the impetus to find a profession where I could work more with my hands. I trained with a florist for several months and attended workshops run by experienced florists. While I was training, I founded Blømeko, my young business specializing in dried flowers. We make arrangements using local and sustainable flowers. We also run a wide range of creative flower workshops where we help attendees make flower arrangements: bouquets, wreaths, accessories, and many other items!

How do you explain consumers' appetite for dried flowers?

It's true that dried flowers have really had a resurgence for several years now! It used to be that when we thought of dried flowers, we'd conjure up images of our grandmothers' dowdy bouquets sitting and gathering dust. Today, dried-flower arrangements have really changed; they are more modern and less structured, and feature graphic foliage elements like dried palm leaves or eucalyptus branches. Another aspect that's breathing new life into dried flowers is the return of very colorful arrangements. For example, there's dried statice, which ranges in color from fuchsia pink to dark purple, midnight-blue echinops, or even craspedia, my little favorites, which make every arrangement pop! I also see two other factors that explain their return. Clients appreciate the durability of these bouquets, which they'll be able to keep for several years. They also see an ecological and economic advantage to buying them. Also, dried flowers are very accessible: they require little maintenance and thus fit in well with our current lifestyles. You don't need to change the water or give the stems a fresh cut!

What is your top-selling item at the store?

My top-selling item is actually a service: creative flower workshops! They are truly a time for creating and passing on knowledge about our dried flowers, which is why I'm in this profession. We welcome in some sixty people a month to workshops. We get people of all different ages—friends, or relatives—who have come to spend a moment together to relax and create!

Can you describe your distribution channels in a bit more detail to us?

I initially launched as an online store where my clients could order bouquets and wreaths, and reserve a spot in a flower workshop. A few months ago, I also opened my first Blømeko store in Annecy, France. It's truly a pleasure to meet my clients face to face and speak with them! We even have a dedicated space for workshops, so we can host large groups on-site. Having a physical and online presence works well. Many people discover the physical store and then keep in contact through social media and the online store.

Where and how do you purchase your raw materials?

When I began, I quickly realized that sourcing dried flowers would be far from the easiest part of my job. Initially I wanted to offer 100 percent French flowers, but I quickly had to scale back my ambitions.

At the start I really relied on the Collectif de la Fleur Française (see page 16), which lists all the different businesses committed to using local flowers, from horticulturists to florists, as well as certain French wholesalers. The collective does incredible work, because it's not always easy to find French growers, not all of whom have an online presence. The directory allowed me to discover numerous, primarily organic, flower farms in France, and I regularly order directly from them.

Increasingly, young flower farms are "going digital," creating websites where you can find the varieties they offer for sale. Many of them offer delivery throughout the country. I also did a great deal of research on my specific region, so I could find out about local growers. I went to meet them and ended up buying fresh flowers from these farms, which I then dried at the store. We are in constant dialogue. I also send them lists of varieties I'd like to have for future harvests.

Despite the establishment of many flower farms over the past three years, the dried-flower industry in France is still not saturated today. The growers I work with are out of stock as of November each year, and you need to wait until the next year's harvest to order again. I now use around 50 percent French flowers, which I supplement with an Italian wholesaler that can offer greater volume the remainder of the year. I ultimately hope to offer 100 percent French flowers, and I'm convinced we'll get there!

Sourcing Flowers

What are the main difficulties of your profession?

I'd say sourcing French dried flowers throughout the year. I have only a little bit of storage space, so I have to spread out my orders, even at the risk of running out of certain flowers. Since dried flowers are durable, I'd like to be able to offer certain bouquets all year, but in reality, stock shortages are all too frequent.

What is your biggest joy?

Seeing my clients arrive at a workshop telling me "I don't know how to do anything with my hands" and then leaving proud of their wreath or bouquet! It's truly satisfying to me to see them build their confidence in their abilities to be creative and make something with their hands!

www.blomeko.fr
@blomeko.floral

CHAPTER 2

THE FLORAL DESIGNER'S TOOLBOX

The floral designer's toolbox holds the equipment that will allow you to work each day. The following list is just a starting point, and you can gather what you need from it and supplement it according to your different projects. Note that it is important to use high-quality tools and to set up a pleasant work environment, which will create the right conditions for making arrangements that are as good as you imagined.

Purchasing tools accounts for a sizeable part of the costs of establishing a floral design business. You should therefore take great care to keep them for as long as possible.

If you are lucky enough to have a dedicated space to work right from the start, really examine your workspace so you can make it functional. Know, however, that many people start off by temporarily setting up

their studio at home. I personally began my adventure in flowers this way. Once a week I would transform my tiny Milan apartment into a studio so I could craft the bouquets that I would offer to my close friends and family. I'd take out all my materials from a large box hidden underneath my bed, and the kitchen table would become my makeshift workbench. On very hot days, it was not rare to find a bouquet of sweet pea wedged between two packages of mozzarella in my fridge!

Over the years, as my practice evolved and my order book filled, my physical work conditions became more professional. Today I have a functional and well-equipped studio, and I'm nostalgic when I think back to those early days!

What Legal Structure Should You Choose When Setting Up Your Business?

Before you register your business with your state, get a tax ID number, and file for the appropriate licenses and permits, you'll need to choose a business structure. You have several possibilities, each of which has its advantages and disadvantages, and the wisest choice depends on your personal situation. So take the time to look at each option carefully, if need be with an accountant or attorney.

To help you decide on a sole proprietorship, a limited liability company (LLC), or another structure, consider especially the amount of personal liability you'll have and the taxes required. It's important to consider whether the legal status allows expenses to be deductible. A floral business generates a lot of expenses.

STARTING YOUR FLORAL DESIGN STUDIO

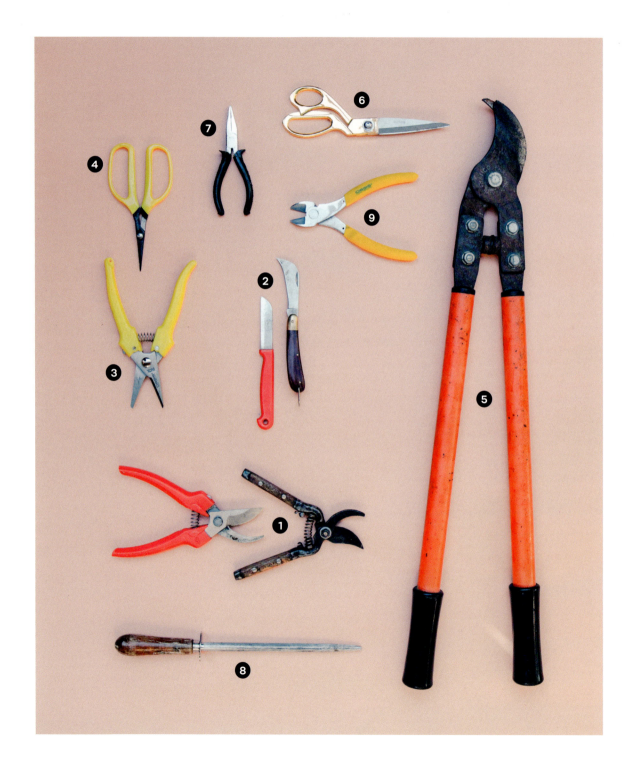

40

Tools for Cutting and Shaping

❶ **Pruning shears:** Used to cut the stems from woody plants. Features curved blades that come to a point in the center.

❷ **Florist's knife or pruning knife:** Also used to cut the stems of flowers. You need a bit of practice to use them without hurting yourself! Out of habit, I prefer these to pruning shears, but it's truly a question of how you work. I use one by the Felco brand.

❸ **Multi-purpose shears:** Straight-edged shears with blades thick enough to cut through floral wire or woody stems.

❹ **Floral scissors:** Often used by people who work with bonsais, because they are smaller and more precise than the tools mentioned above. I personally use them to touch up finished arrangements and cut delicate stems or flowers that are hard to access.

❺ **Pruners:** Cuts heftier branches, up to about 1.75 in. (45 mm) in diameter.

❻ **Fabric shears:** Essential for neatly cutting ribbons and fabric used to top off arrangements. Be careful not to give in to the temptation to use them for anything other than fabric, since the blades wear down quickly.

❼ **Round nose pliers:** Used for working with floral wire or chicken wire.

❽ **Sharpening steel:** For honing sharp tools, which become dull when used over time.

❾ **Wire cutter:** A tool for cutting chicken wire or small- and medium-width wire stems.

Tools for Hanging, Fastening, and Gluing

❶ Raffia: A natural and biodegradable solution for tying up bouquets.

❷ Twine: Used to tie all kinds of plants together.

❸ Floral tape: Waterproof, adhesive tape for securing balls of chicken wire in containers. Take care to use it sparingly, since it is neither biodegradable nor reusable.

❹ Glue gun: Essential for jury-rigging containers or gluing on decorative elements.

❺ Floral sticky clay: Green adhesive paste, which I primarily use for attaching a kenzan to its vase. May be reused many times.

❻ Fishing line: Clear line for hanging lightweight cloud arrangements.

❼ Metal wire and flat fastener: Used to hang the heaviest cloud arrangements.

❽ Plastic cable ties: One of my biggest unresolved dilemmas to date! Cable ties are very practical during events, because they can be used to quickly and completely secure different components. However, it is still a single-use, plastic item . . .

❾ Velcro: A more eco-friendly alternative to cable ties for assembling certain elements. It has the advantage of being reusable, although I find it to be less secure.

❿ Floral tape: Strip of wax-coated crepe paper used to create all kinds of tiny, detailed items, such as boutonnieres and flower crowns.

⓫ Kenzan: A Japanese tool used in the art of *ikebana*. It is placed at the bottom of a vase and allows the flowers to stay upright.

⓬ Wire stems: Sold in bundles of different widths, and used to fasten different components; may be cut.

⓭ Paddle wire: Can be used to quickly tie different elements together.

⓮ Chicken wire: Flexible and infinitely reusable wire sold by the roll in various dimensions, galvanized, or covered with a green plastic film. I prefer the green, which is more flexible and easier to cut. If you opt for the galvanized version, consider wearing protective gloves when cutting them.

⓯ Clear adhesive tape: Useful for hanging lightweight elements.

STARTING YOUR FLORAL DESIGN STUDIO

Tools for Watering and Maintaining Moisture

THE CLASSICS

❶ Flower bucket: A black plastic bucket that allows flowers to stay submerged. Be sure to allow your buckets to dry thoroughly before packing in the flowers; otherwise you'll risk having a hard time separating them from one another later! I frequently use these in ways other than those for which they were intended, flipping them over to use as a support when I make centerpieces: they provide me with a comfortable working height.

❷ Watering can: Ideally, you'd have several sizes, for addressing the various situations and needs that arise.

❸ Spray bottle: Effective when you need to refresh plants at the installation site.

❹ Wash bottle: Allows you to precisely pour water into hard-to-access containers.

❺ Flower water tubes: Small plastic tubes with perforated, reusable caps. I use these in many different situations.

❻ Grave spikes: This product is very practical and allows you to keep the flowers in water in large-scale structures such as arches. Its shape allows it to be speared and then placed upright in the chicken wire.

❼ Planters: Perfect for walkways or ground gardens. Planters often have drainage holes: to make them waterproof, I plug up the holes with a glue gun. To elevate a less than beautiful plastic model, you can simply hide the sides with natural moss.

STARTING YOUR FLORAL DESIGN STUDIO

UNIQUE ADDITIONS

❶ **Cylindrical glass or ceramic vase:** A classic model used for arrangements featuring upright, rather than trailing flowers. Available in numerous heights and widths. Pictured is a very simple glass cylinder along with a fanciful stoneware model made by ceramicist Théo Tourne.

Square or rectangular vase: Very practical for making standard arrangements with large blooms, such as peonies or hydrangeas. The stems easily fill up the corners.

❷ **Compote vase:** I use a mesh or kenzan technique (see page 100) for these containers. They allow you to create ethereal, free-form arrangements. The yellow piece pictured here is by Raawii and comes in several colors. Stéphane Raymond of Atelier Setsuko made the taller beige model.

❸ **Bowl:** A variation on the compote vase, but without the foot. The three pieces shown here were made by Stéphane Raymond of Atelier Setsuko.

❹ **Medici-type vase:** Practical for oversized arrangements. I line it with a plastic bucket and place chicken wire inside.

❺ **Opaline bud vase:** Delicate glass vase with a dainty neck, available in pretty pastel colors. I'm growing my collection with flea market and yard sale finds.

❻ **Cut glass:** I adore the retro feel of these. I've spent long hours searching through yard sale tables to build my collection!

❼ **Various vintage carafes:** I use groups of whiskey or cognac carafes as centerpieces, placing one or two flowers inside of each one.

The Perfect Container

As far as fanciful vases are concerned, I'm in the habit of bargain hunting and building collections of various categories: porcelain, stoneware, brass, opaline glass, cut glass, etc. Keep in mind that any container can become a very pretty vase: a soup tureen, a wicker basket, or even a shoe lined with a waterproof bottom! I also truly enjoy working with ceramicists with whom I can place specific orders. You'll find references to some of my go-to people in this chapter.

STARTING YOUR FLORAL DESIGN STUDIO

48

Transport Materials

❶ **Carabiner clips and hooks:** Practical in many situations, especially for securing arrangements inside your vehicle during transport to the delivery location.

❷ **Tie-down strap:** Also essential for securing your materials in the vehicle.

❸ **Cardboard boxes:** I never buy these. I collect and reuse the ones I receive. They are very useful for transporting arrangements to the installation site or for wedging in between arrangements so that they don't move inside the vehicle.

❹ **Rolling plant caddy:** Allows large arrangements to be transported short distances.

❺ **Plastic box and crate:** To securely carry your materials and arrangements to the installation site.

❻ **Vehicle:** If you rent a van, be sure to make your reservation well in advance so that you don't end up in trouble a few days before installation day. Additionally, really think about what volume you need for the items to be moved.

❼ **Cloth:** To protect the flowers and wrap vases for transport.

❽ **Bungee cord:** As with tie-down straps, useful for keeping flowers and materials inside the vehicle.

❾ **Dolly with wheels:** Necessary for efficiently moving heavy items.

STARTING YOUR FLORAL DESIGN STUDIO

50

Materials for Decorating and Wrapping Arrangements

❶ Ribbon: Decorative tie. May be made of different materials, such as velvet, satin, grosgrain, or muslin. I personally have a penchant for grosgrain. I love everything about it, particularly its retro feel. For wedding bouquets, I love to get hold of some naturally dyed velvet or silk chiffon ribbon.

❷ Brown kraft paper: Very sturdy paper for wrapping up bouquets; gives a natural, rustic look to your packaging.

❸ Colored paper: More sophisticated than kraft paper. It comes in various colors and weights.

❸ Stiff paper bag: I use these to wrap and transport wedding bouquets or smaller arrangements, like centerpieces. It allows items to be moved securely.

❹ Fancy note cards: For writing nice messages to clients!

❺ Ball-head straight pins: Useful for attaching ribbon or a note card.

Items for Setting Up Your Studio

Worktable: Choose one that is a bit higher than hip level so you can be comfortable standing there. Your back will thank you! It may be useful to add wheels so you can easily move it should you need space to make larger arrangements.

Small rolling cart: Practical for arranging the tools you use most, which you always want to have within arm's length (pruning knife, scissors, wire, etc.). I bought mine from IKEA.

Wall shelves: Allow you to gain considerable space, not to mention store all of your materials. I personally tend to amass a countless number of things "that I might use one day." They range from the pretty blueish stone I found during a hike to a strange vase I unearthed at a yard sale—so I need a lot of space to store all my finds.

Storage bins: For sliding under the table and onto shelves. You can place the tools you use least often inside them. Choose clear ones so that you can see what they contain with a quick glance.

Kraft paper dispenser: As its name suggests, used to make it easier to roll out a sheet of kraft paper.

Water supply: Yes! Flowers need water! It is therefore important that you have easy access to a water source. Try for stainless steel or plastic sinks. If a vase slides out of your hands, there will be less chance of it breaking than in a ceramic or stone sink!

Cold room or air conditioning: It's a thorny question from an environmental standpoint, but it may be necessary depending on your work location. I personally am lucky enough to have a temperate studio that does not need to be cooled down to preserve the flowers. Your call.

Light: Good lighting is essential for making your flower arrangements and allowing you to play with their colors and shapes. Unfortunately, very few of us will be lucky enough to work under an magnificent glass roof bathed in natural light! I invested in LED ceiling fixtures, which use minimal energy, provide good light, and last longer than classic bulbs.

CHAPTER 3

THE BASIC PRINCIPLES OF FLORAL DESIGN

In the winter of 2017, I pushed open the door of a charming small boutique in West Milan that I had been looking at longingly for several months. The space was around 215.28 sq. ft. (20 m²), and literally caving under the weight of the flowers. All the way at the back of the room, barely visible among the plants, was Gaetano, the owner, and his employee Samantha. Proudly displayed above the counter were the multiple "International Floral Designer" diplomas he'd earned over the years. Mustering up a level of courage I had never had before, I offered my services.

At the time, I was still working at an advertising agency, and I did not have any experience with flowers. I had just enrolled in a virtual program to prepare for the Florist Occupational Certificate at CNED (French National Center for Distance Education), and I was boning up on the theory portion of the curriculum in my free time. To my great surprise, Gaetano, who was no doubt intrigued by my uncommon profile, agreed to take me under his wing. We worked together for one year at his store, Fiorinmente. I learned the basic rules of flower arranging from him (and know that he was a stickler for rules!). I then combined that knowledge with additional training from other talented professionals in the industry. I worked on the most ambitious projects with Massimo Pilastro and Davide Bandiera, the team behind the very beautiful Milan floral design studio MADA. We provided floral arrangements for lavish weddings in gorgeous villas on the banks of Lake Como, elegant window displays and showrooms for high-end labels, and VIP dinners for Fashion Week shows. Working with them taught me how to think big! To this day, I'm still refining all that know-how I learned from them in my projects at Nebbia Studio.

I must confess that I am a lot more flexible than my very first teacher as concerns flower arrangement theory. I would even go so far as to say that I sometimes take a devilish pleasure in bending the rules. Nevertheless, I think it's important to know and master the rules, and *then* knowingly bend them.

The principles I've introduced in this chapter apply regardless of the type of arrangement you are choosing to make, whether it's a simple small bouquet or a large-scale arch. However, I suggest you experiment on smaller pieces before embarking on more ambitious projects. In my opinion, a centerpiece is an excellent place to start.

Choosing Flowers

When designing arrangements, we can sometimes feel a bit flummoxed by nature's countless possibilities. The tools I've given you will allow you to get a clearer idea, so that you can dive right into making gorgeous arrangements.

CATEGORIES OF FLOWERS

I love to draw an analogy to film when discussing different categories of flowers; the image generally speaks for itself. The idea is to imagine you are a casting director who is going to look for actors and actresses to play in an upcoming film. Our "cast list" will include all or part of the following elements.

The Basic Principles of Floral Design

GARDEN ROSE   DAHLIA   POPPY

COSMOS   SCABIOSA   CLEMATIS

- The main flower: This is the star, the leading actress of our arrangement, and she is impressive, dazzling, and prized. This is the scene-stealing focal flower, and it is often the costliest one in the group. The rest of the arrangement will take shape around it. Some examples of focal flowers are dahlias, garden roses, poppies, bearded irises, or peonies.

- Complementary flowers: They have a supporting role and are smaller and more discreet. They are nonetheless essential to the arrangement and their presence reinforces that of the focal flower. Flowers such as cosmos, scabiosa, or clematis might be used for this purpose.

- Filler flowers: These are the extras, the crowd in the background providing some volume to the scene; we tend to notice very little about their specific features. Filler flowers are there to create heft. Statice, broom, or chamomile might be used here.

STARTING YOUR FLORAL DESIGN STUDIO

STATICE

BROOM

CHAMOMILE

FLOWERING CHERRY TREE BRANCHES

variety, or of so-called "rustic" arrangements, made from florets that are often considered secondary flowers. These arrangements don't have any defined pecking order among the different plants used.

FOLIAGE

At Nebbia Studio, I chose to develop a very colorful style with very little foliage. I do incorporate bits of greenery, but I prefer to showcase the flowers, highlighting their textures and colors. But really it depends on what you like!

Incidentally, foliage can be very useful in large-scale arrangements for creating volume and building a base structure, since in comparison to cut flowers, it's generally well priced. Greenery can even be completely free if you are lucky enough to live in the country and have a backyard. It also offers a diverse range of materials and shapes.

Here are a few examples of foliage that I really like.

- Spindle: Also known as bishop's cap, it has green foliage that turns orangey red in fall. Its bright-pink and orange fruit indeed look like tiny caps. I really like using it in centerpieces.

- The cameo: This is the flash appearance of a star! A delicate and surprising flower that pops up here and there in our arrangement. It catches our eye for a quick moment. A flowering cherry tree branch might serve this purpose.

If you choose to incorporate all these kinds of flowers, you'll be rewarded with a very rich and dynamic arrangement, although of course other combinations are possible. I'm thinking in particular of so-called "single-flower" arrangements, where you use a single

- Abelia: Branches are dotted with numerous tiny leaves. It is in the honeysuckle family, and a delicately scented pale-pink blossom complements its dark-green leaves. I love to use it in bridal bouquets.

- 'Royal Purple' *Cotinus coggygria*: I love its dark, brownish/wine color. Its oval leaves hold their shape and stand upright without being in water. In summer it boasts a delicate, downy flower. Nice and full, it's perfect for large-scale floral arrangements.

- Sage: I particularly love the velvety texture of its leaves and their soft color. I buy it by the pot and use it in low centerpieces.

- Asparagus fern: With its pure green color, my favorite variety is the Asparagus umbellatus. Its feathery leaves are very decorative and are perfect in bouquets.

ABELIA

'ROYAL PURPLE' *COTINUS COGGYGRIA*

SPINDLE

SAGE

ASPARAGUS

The Golden Rules of Foliage Foraging

If you want to forage for foliage in nature, you must abide by a few principles.

1. Find out which species are protected in your area, and abide by the current rules that pertain to them.

2. Request authorization to pick plants from the owner of the premises (whether it is a private piece of land or a public space).

3. Use proper tools and make clean cuts to respect and preserve the health of the plant.

4. Be frugal and take only what you need.

5. Determine a purchase price, because while foraged foliage is certainly free, the time you spend gathering it should be billed to the client.

TEXTURES

In this context, texture does not correspond to the feeling you get when you touch the plants, but to what their appearance evokes from our senses. This impacts the style of your creations and provides very interesting contrasts. Working with texture in floral arrangements is similar to how painters work with texture in their canvases, with one specific difference: painters have all the tools they need to allow them to change the consistency of the painting at their disposal, while florists can influence consistency only through their choice of raw materials. By studying the specific characteristics of the plants we use, we can create interesting and aesthetically pleasing combinations and groupings.

Types of Floral Textures

This list cites just a few of the floral textures you can use to add depth to your arrangements. You can expand it as you see what works for you.

- Silky: soft, delicate surface. Examples include gladiola, sweet pea, 'Café au lait' dahlia.
- Metallic : hard, shiny, and smooth surface. Examples include anthurium, fritillaria, tulips.
- Rustic: coarse, irregular surface. Examples include eryngium, *Ammi*, amaranth.
- Velvety: soft and plush surface. Examples include celosia, sage, poppy.
- Feathery: ethereal, uneven surface. Examples include *Cotinus*, pampas grass, astilbe.

The Basic Principles of Floral Design

I love to create voluminous arrangements with multiple layers of textures. You can introduce texture through several different elements. While flowers and foliage can serve as the base of the project, you can also add unexpected components such as berries, branches, or fruits.

There are some very specific cases when playing with textures is, for me, the most interesting part: for example, in monochromatic arrangements where you want to match the container or the environment. Texture adds depth and intensity to monochromatic arrangements. Take the case of a completely white bouquet.

Pairing the silky texture of a garden rose with the rustic effect of baby's breath will make for an eye-catching bouquet.

Visual consistency in an arrangement is more important than the flowers selected. Indeed, texture allows you to create a connection between the group of flowers and what surrounds them. You can work with similarities; for example, by livening up a smooth metallic vase with a flower that brings that aspect to mind, such as anthurium. Or you can play with contrasts, by placing a feathery plant such as *Cotinus* in front of a large curtain of velvety flowers.

RUSTIC

FEATHERY

METALLIC

SILKY

VELVETY

Making a Successful Floral Arrangement

VOLUME

Whether it's a bouquet, centerpiece, arch, or another small- or large-scale floral piece, every project should be in proper proportion so that the result is well balanced. Achieving this comes from properly working with volume.

The first thing to understand is that an arrangement is three-dimensional. This concept may be obvious, but it's sometimes difficult to master.

The starting premise is this: a floral arrangement must always be designed in terms of height, width, and depth.

- Height: The verticality of the arrangement, its size. For example, for a floral arrangement done in a vase, theoretically, the container should visually account for one-third of the total arrangement.

- Width is the horizontality of the arrangement, how far it extends to the left and right.

- Depth is the general volume of the arrangement. It consists of successive layers from the front to the back of the arrangement. These layers themselves have variable heights. Depth is often the concept that requires the most practice to be mastered. Indeed, when you start out, there is a tendency to place all the plants along the same line. The bouquet then has a very heavy look to it. With experience, you'll learn how to deconstruct it and create movement.

ELEMENTS OF VOLUME

In addition to the different sizes we have discussed, there is the issue of shape, lines, positive and negative space, and the rhythm or flow of the arrangement; all these concepts will contribute to the final volume.

- **Shape:** Before even starting the arrangement, you must determine the general shape. Will it be round, oval, triangular, in a semicircle ... there are so many possibilities! You can make it symmetrical, to give it a more classic look, or asymmetrical, for a more modern flair.

- **Lines:** How your plants are placed within the arrangement. Each direction results in a different feel. Vertical lines create a sense of strength and solidity, diagonal lines provide dynamic movement, curves add elegance, and trailing lines give a sense of weightiness.

- **Full and empty space:** Unless you want to create a compact, uniform mass, it may be useful for you to master these principles. Full or "positive" spaces represent the areas occupied by the plants and the containers. Empty or "negative" space refers to the places that are deliberately left untouched. A good balance between positive and negative space prevents viewers from getting bored with too sparse an arrangement, or from getting lost in something too busy. It helps convey the rhythm of the bouquet.

- **Rhythm:** Just as in a musical arrangement, floral arrangement requires rhythm to be pleasant and consistent. This rhythm helps convey the performative aspect of flower design. It allows us to guide the eye toward important elements, and then allows the viewer to get lost in the details of the work. It's a voyage through flowers, foliage, and textures, where placement has been carefully decided. Many components can set the rhythm: different heights, colors, groupings of a single variety of flower, or groupings of flowers with the same texture.

BALANCE AND PROPORTION

There are two concepts that are interesting to understand when working with balance and proportion in flower arrangement: the golden ratio and the rule of thirds.

The Golden Ratio

This first rule is perhaps the hardest to comprehend. "Divine proportion" or "the golden ratio" is considered to be the universal formula for beauty and harmony, which is based on an aesthetic of proportions. The architect Vitruve defined it as this: "For a space, divided into unequal parts, to appear pleasant and aesthetically pleasing, there must be the same ratio between the smallest part and the biggest part as between the biggest part and the whole."

This is used as the ultimate point of reference in disciplines ranging from painting to architecture, as well as photography and music.

We can apply this notion concretely in floral design, by actually composing the famous Fibonacci spiral that resulted from the geometric application of the Fibonacci sequence.

The flowers are then placed into the spiral, allowing the eye to grasp the harmony of the components.

FIBONACCI SPIRAL APPLIED TO AN ARRANGEMENT

The Rule of Thirds

The rule of thirds also allows you to obtain a nice visual balance. The basic principle is this: to provide a visual feel of harmony in an arrangement, you need to see one-third container, and two-thirds contents. Therefore, the vase should account for only one-third of the height, with the plants occupying the remaining two-thirds.

Not only is this rule relevant when placing flowers in a vase, but it can also be applied to many other ratios of proportion in arrangements:

- The ratio between the floral arrangement and its environment: If you are placing an imposing arrangement in a room, make sure to flower only two-thirds of the length of the room, leaving the remaining third empty.

- The ratio between the flowers and their stems in a bouquet: The height of the stems beneath the tie should represent one-third the bouquet's total height.

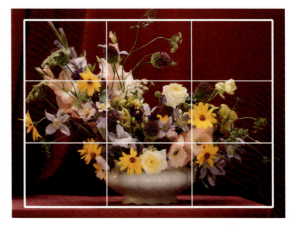

RULE OF THIRDS APPLIED TO AN ARRANGEMENT

Understanding Color Harmony

Color is one of the first pieces of information that catches your eye when you look at a flower arrangement. Knowing how to pair colors is therefore one of the first skills to achieve a balanced result. Playing with different shades is truly a pleasure for me, and I think it is important and worthy of my time to work on color palettes for each of my projects.

Your color analysis may be limited to the flowers themselves or may consider the various other elements surrounding them: vase, tablecloth, furniture, walls, etc.

THE COLOR WHEEL

The color wheel is a tool that allows you to order how colors are represented. It was invented by Isaac Newton in the seventeenth century. Colors are grouped according to a specific order. They are classified into three groups: primary colors, secondary colors, and tertiary colors.

Primary colors are the bases from which you can mix and create all the colors that exist in nature. They are yellow, blue, and magenta.

Secondary colors are obtained by mixing two primary colors together, resulting in orange, green, and violet.

Last, tertiary colors are formed by mixing equal parts of a secondary color with one of the two primary colors composing it. They can be grouped into six shades: purple, turquoise, indigo, ocher, acid green, and vermillion.

COLOR PAIRINGS

In floral arrangement, an eye for color develops through practice. At the beginning, it can be very intimidating to pair colors, and you wonder if your chosen pairings are harmonious.

While I do encourage you to experiment and invent bold palettes, we'll review different possible color pairings according to tried-and-true rules. I recommend that you start practicing with the simplest combinations. Once you feel comfortable with the process, you can experiment with bolder combinations.

Warm and Cool Colors

As with texture, the idea of heat to define a color corresponds to a visual sensation. When you draw a line to the center of the color wheel, between yellow and purple, you'll see the cool range on the right, and the warm range on the left. Warm colors all contain a bit of yellow, while cool colors contain a bit of blue.

A simple solution to avoid any blunders is to arrange and pair flowers that all belong to the same temperature class.

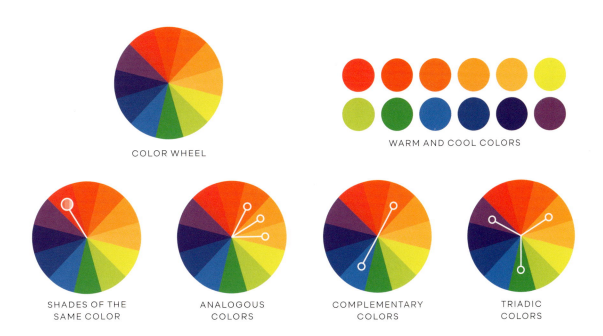

STARTING YOUR FLORAL DESIGN STUDIO

EXPERT ADVICE

Cécile Bertin, Cili Brtn, artist and interior color specialist

*Once you have chosen your color palette, it will also be important to know how to describe it, particularly when justifying your choices to clients.
To help you find the right words, I got some advice from Cécile, who assists architects and individuals in creating harmonious color stories to enhance spaces, showcase architectural lines, and create spaces within a space. She also collaborates with textile and lifestyle brands to create harmonious color palettes.*

Describing a color is far from simple, given that each person perceives colors differently. Here are some key points to help you describe and evoke the desired feel, using certain shades and nuances.

There are different registers that help professionals show tones and shades, as well as their balance, intensity, and their nuance.

- **Technical:** (luminosity, saturation... classification tools)
- **Cultural:** (names of historical colors)
- **Sensorial:** hearing (bold colors), touch (cool tone, fresh color), taste (spicy red), smell (fruity)
- **Parallels, or even comparisons to plants** (orange, lemon), foods (chocolate, caramel), animal life (salmon, chamois), different aspects of nature (aqua, sunrise), precious substances (gold, ruby, emerald)
- **Feelings** (harmony, sweet, joyous)

Let's take the example of blue: "the color of my dreams," as Miró used to say. Blue elicits a feeling of freedom, of infinity, like the ocean, which is clear on the surface, and so intense in its depth. It can be simultaneously soothing, romantic and somber, silent and mysterious at nightfall, or even sweet like a pretty spring day. We can also refer to the freshness of a mint candy, or the artwork of Yves Klein, which describes a luminous blue...

www.cilibrtn.com

Ombré

Ombré is an easy technique to learn, and can provide a soft, uniform look to arrangements. It consists of choosing one color and then using different shades of that color gradient. These different tones will provide depth to the arrangement. Just like working with cool and warm colors, ombré is an excellent technique for beginners.

Analogous Colors

To use a range of analogous colors, choose three colors that are next to each other on the color wheel. The look will be quite soft yet have more contrast than an ombré.

Complementary Colors

These are colors that are opposite one another on the color wheel. Pairing them allows you to create a very strong contrast while still maintaining good visual harmony.

Triadic Colors

To find triadic colors, draw an equilateral triangle on the color wheel. The colors in question are at the end of its three angles. This color pairing is bolder and quite dynamic.

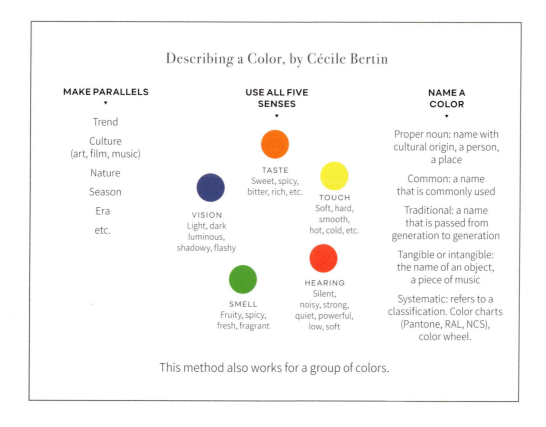

CHAPTER 4

THE MAIN STAGES OF A FLORAL DESIGN PROJECT

Merely knowing how to make floral arrangements is not enough to make a living out of your passion. You must also know how to manage the projects you are assigned and how to listen to your client. These steps will require your creativity, which is essential for making a mood board you can later use for your proposal. However, you'll also need good business negotiation skills. Likewise, installation requires a certain organizational sense, and managerial skills, if you work with a team.

Each floral design project is a blank slate, to be executed differently depending on your various roles.

The required qualifications extend well beyond simply working with flowers, and in my opinion, that's one of the most motivating aspects of our profession! I was able to familiarize myself with most of these related skills before becoming a florist. When I then changed professions, I was able to primarily focus on working with flowers, which allowed me to save precious time.

If you are just learning about these topics as you read this book, don't panic! A bit of practice and organization will allow you to successfully complete your projects and confidently turn your passion into a profession.

Defining the Project

THE FIRST DISCUSSION WITH THE CLIENT

Whether it's for a wedding, a brand photo shoot, an installation for a boutique, or any other floral project, the first conversation with the client is very important. During this conversation, you must be able to grasp the scope of the project and determine whether it's right for you. You don't necessarily have to submit a proposal just because you're available on the required dates!

Introductions

Take the time to introduce yourself, explain how you work, and express your values. For example, if you use 100 percent flowers from a certain region, this would be a good time to explain your process.

Talk about recent projects you've worked on that are similar to the potential project, and start introducing the idea of rates. If you've set a minimum budget for your work, don't hesitate to say so at this point. Your time and your client's time are precious, so it's pointless to devote more energy to the project if you are not on the same wavelength.

If, after this first phase, you wish to do business together, it is then time to start collecting whatever information you feel will be useful to you! By the end of this conversation, you should have your clients' contact information, along with all the information you'll need to work on a proposal.

Ambiance and Style

The first series of questions will address the ambiance and style your clients are seeking to create.

- Do they have a specific idea of what they want?
- Are they giving you free rein on style and colors, or have they already decided on these aspects?
- Have they put together any ideas on Pinterest?
- Have they done a brief?

Try to get as many details as possible.

Budget

The second series of questions will be financial in nature. Ideally, you'll get an idea of their budget so you can provide an appropriate proposal.

In the case of floral design projects for brands or businesses, it's relatively easy to get this kind of information. These clients are often at least somewhat familiar with the price of flowers or know the budget allocated for this line item of their project. When dealing with individuals, however, things are a bit more delicate, particularly when it's for their wedding. While wedding planners are familiar with market rates, brides and grooms might not be, in which case you'll have to be patient and educate your client.

While it may be the thorniest of subjects, knowing the client's budget is essential for being able to make an appropriate proposal. This will both prevent you from disappointing them with a proposal that is not elaborate enough, and avoid causing panic with a proposal that is way over budget.

YOUR LOGO **CLIENT CONTACT SHEET**

TYPE OF PROJECT
Event, wedding, photo shoot, film shoot, etc.

DATE OF PROJECT
Enter date

CLIENT INFORMATION

NAME	*Client's name*
TELEPHONE	*Client's telephone number*
EMAIL	*Client's email address*
LOCATION	*Enter link to website of location where the event will be held*
FLOWERS NEEDED	*Precisely describe client's request*
PROPOSALS MADE	*Note what you proposed to client during interview*
MOOD BOARD	*Enter link to client's Pinterest board, if they've made one*
COLORS AND STYLE	*Note the colors envisioned, style, theme*
BUDGET	*Enter client's budget*

SAMPLE CONTACT SHEET

THE MOOD BOARD

At Nebbia Studio, I primarily work on custom, original projects. Every proposal I make to a client is unique. The mood board is the point of departure that allows me to structure the project and give it direction.

The Basic Principle

In the context of floral design, a mood board is a set of images that allows you to provide a vision for creative proposals, including a project's style, colors, and textures. It's the only visual reference that the client will have before the flower arrangements are delivered. It allows you to plan easily and to get a general idea of the result. When you make a mood board, you are also establishing a powerful means of communication, which allows you to convey ideas and feelings. You should consider it a true business tool.

Before I begin, I should be able to answer three questions.

1. What message do I want to convey? This involves providing a theme or an ambiance, or telling a specific story. In some cases, the client brief already contains numerous useful details. In others, I have to build every element of the presentation. Inspiration can be found anywhere: painting, architecture, sculpture, fashion, design, cinema, there's no limit!

2. What floral elements do you want to showcase? This is not about finding pictures to illustrate every floral piece that I will then propose in the estimate, but rather about highlighting the most important ones and presenting the seasonal flowers available at the time of the project.

3. Who is my client? When I'm able to really understand who my client is, I'm better able to meet their expectations. If my client is a brand, I'll learn about its history, its DNA, and its values. If it's a couple who is getting married, I'll get to know their taste and lifestyle. The contact sheet on page 71 is a good place to start.

I then organize the responses I've collected into a dedicated worksheet and start assembling my mood board.

In Practice

My mood boards always contain two elements:

- The color palette: this sets the tone and evokes emotion.
- Images: these form the basis for the concept that is presented to the client.

The first stage is therefore to define the color palette. Does your client have a very specific idea of what they want, or are they giving you free rein? In both cases, it's important to visually show the palette so you can be sure you are moving in the right direction. To help you decide on a color chart, you can rely on the color theory we saw on pages 64 to 67. I personally love to use this as my point of departure and then allow myself a bit of stylistic license.

There are various tools online that allow you to create seamless palettes. Use search terms such as "color palette generator" to try some.

The second stage consists of conducting visual research. The initial goal is to collect all images that correspond to the ambiance I want to create. I then sort them and select the ones that work best together. I mainly use Pinterest and Instagram for my visual research. I set up topic-specific charts through these two platforms.

Should You Bill for the Mood Board?

With individuals, especially where weddings are concerned, the matter of whether or not to bill for the mood board is an area I believe could stand some improvement. Every florist I have worked for in the past has buried the time used to create the mood board into the total estimate, without making it a clear line item. I do the same, but I'm not entirely satisfied with it. In fact, I think it erases some of the value of an aspect of our work that is essential and extremely creative.

Moreover, if the agreement isn't signed, the time spent on the mood board is lost.

One practice that might be worth exploring is what architects do when they bill for a project study and the drafting of the initial plans, stages that are somewhat similar to that of a florist creating a mood board. After that first work product, the client decides whether to keep collaborating with the provider on the project and move forward with the work.

Doing it that way isn't the norm (to my knowledge) in our business, except on very large-scale projects at extremely large floral design studios. Who knows if our individual clients would accept this type of process!

With professional clients, it's a bit different. For example, for a photo shoot project where flowers would be at the center of the artistic direction and you'd be asked to propose several creative ideas, it would be simpler to create a line item in your quotes.

SAMPLE MOOD BOARD

I use Pinterest to do specific research using keywords, just as I would with a classic search engine. I use Instagram a bit differently, however. On this platform, I've built a true library of images for myself over the years. I save images that specifically caught my attention, and arrange them by categories for later use.

I always select four different types of images. (See an example on the previous page.) It's an effective combination that I like and that works well.

- Inspiration images: These are not necessarily images that represent flowers, but ones that I've chosen because they evoke a certain emotion or point to a detail of the project. They also match the color palette so I can keep things visually consistent.
- Portraits of flowers: I select some of the flowers I'm planning to put in my arrangements.
- Images of floral pieces that I want to make for the event.
- Images of materials and textures.

As you'll see, making this type of document takes time! It is therefore important to really gauge how serious your client is before you dive in. If necessary, you can begin with a more minimal version containing a single color palette and two or three images that inspire you, to set the tone. You can then explain to the client that you'll work on a more detailed version, if they wish, once the quote has been approved.

Despite this investment in time, a nice mood board can give you a considerable advantage over competitors who do not offer one, and it tips the scales in your favor on certain projects. So it is up to you to evaluate on a case-by-case basis whether this work will be worth the time you'll spend on it.

SITE VISIT AND STAGING AT THE LOCATION

As you work on the mood board, depending on the type of project you're working on, you may need to visit the event location. The information you collect on-site can have an impact on your final quote.

For example, if you want to flower a staircase, you'll need to know its length, and consider the width of the steps and the surrounding area. This will allow you to determine which type of plants will work best, along with the necessary volume, which are essential elements for calculating the price of the installation. If it's not possible to plan a visit (for example, due to tight time constraints, very long distances, or a budget that does not allow for that kind of travel), contact the people who manage the space to get as much information as possible.

The main goals of the site visit are:

- To get clear and precise information about access: Can I park vehicles for unloading? Is it possible to use dollies to move materials? Is there an elevator? This information might impact the number of people you plan on having for the installation, and therefore also impact the quote. For example, if you have to park your vehicle really far from the event space and it's not possible to use a dolly due to stairs, you'll need to plan on having more hands!
- Determine where your base camp will be located, if you'll need to make flower arrangements on-site on the day of installation (I'll come back to this on page 82).
- Scout out the areas to be decorated, take their exact measurements, and take pictures.

Once the quote has been approved, I organize all this information in a site visit sheet. I've provided a sample of it (opposite). I then create a special folder on my computer that has the name of the location. I place this sheet in the folder, along with photos of the estab-

The Main Stages of a Floral Design Project

YOUR LOGO		SITE VISIT SHEET
	GENERAL INFORMATION	
Name of location and website	Name of location and link to website	
ADDRESS	Exact address of location	
MANAGER NAME	Name of your on-site contact	
TELEPHONE NUMBER	Your contact's telephone number	
EMAIL	Your contact's email address	
	TECHNICAL INFORMATION	
ACCESS TIMES	Are there specific access times?	
VEHICLE ACCESSIBILITY	Are there parking areas? Is the installation area close to the parking area?	
BUILDING ACCESSIBILITY	Is there an entry code? Is there an elevator or freight elevator?	
WATER SOURCE	Where is the water source available to me during the installation located?	
ELECTRICITY	Where is the outlet available to me during the installation located?	
EXPOSURE	What time does the sun set and where?	
DISTANCE FROM STUDIO	How many miles (kilometers) is it from the studio to the location? What is the travel time?	

SAMPLE SITE VISIT SHEET

lishment. It's a very practical process, and if I ever end up working in one of these locations again, I can refer to this virtual library.

DESIGNING YOUR FLORAL MOCK-UP

Depending on what type of project you are working on, it might also be useful to do a mock-up. This step consists of drawing or outlining some of your most important floral pieces so that your client can get an idea of the end result. It's an additional tool that will help support the project. I offer the service as an option, and then incorporate it into the quote, estimating the time spent completing the drawing.

I use the application Procreate on my iPad and draw directly on my photos from the site visit with an Apple Pencil. Although it does take a bit of time to get to know the tool, understand how the interface works, and learn what functionalities are available, it's a very intuitive program. To help you get started, the web has a ton of video tutorials that will allow you to get the basics down easily. Procreate is a tool you pay for, but it's very inexpensive.

SAMPLE OF A MOCK-UP DONE WITH PROCREATE

I tried several other types of mock-ups before settling on this software. My goal was to find the one that was most suitable and least time consuming. Below are some examples of techniques that will allow you to create mock-ups.

1. Summarize the type of information in a diagram: This type of mock-up allows you to efficiently convey what the main elements of your decor are and how you imagine placing them. It has the benefit of being quick to do, although it does not offer any specific creative and stylistic interest, and is therefore less representative of the end result.

2. Do a freehand sketch: This technique also has the benefit of being fairly quick. It provides a few more details than a simple diagram and allows you to easily plan. Be careful though; if you are not very comfortable drawing, this could put you in a less favorable position. In that case, choose a diagram, which is a more neutral option.

3. Call in an illustrator: For certain projects where your client is expecting you to provide high precision and a very comprehensive mood board, it could be worth using an illustrator, whose work can supplement your ideas and provide beautiful added value to your project. This is a line item that could be provided as an option for your client to approve in the quote.

THE QUOTE

You've understood your client's needs since the first conversation, and you've begun to make the project official, using images to build a partial or full mood board. You might even have familiarized yourself with the event location. The only thing left to do is write up the quote.

Trust Yourself and Your Rates

Oh, quotes! I remember myself trembling and hesitant when it came time to write my first one. It had been ready for two days when I finally decided to click the "Send" button! While on the one hand, I was comfortable with my rates on the basis of the suggestions that had been made, I was also completely paralyzed by the fear of offending my client, who, from what I could surmise, might not be expecting such a high number. I was unnerved by the (completely fabricated) risk of losing out on the work opportunity.

In actuality, the experience allowed me to understand that when we discuss budgets with our clients, we need to put our emotions aside and focus on the facts alone. You have to explain why you charge the rates that you do, stay professional, and always be open to discussion.

The Main Stages of a Floral Design Project

YOUR LOGO

NAME OF YOUR BUSINESS
ADDRESS
TELEPHONE NO.
EMAIL
BUSINESS ID NO.

Today's Date

QUOTE NUMBER 000

CLIENT'S FIRST AND LAST NAME
ADDRESS
TELEPHONE NO.
EMAIL

NAME AND DATE OF PROJECT

Item	Quantity	Unit Price, All Taxes Included	Amount Before Taxes	Amount, All Taxes Included
BRIDE'S BOUQUET *Bride's bouquet in a natural and deconstructed style, medium size, composed of seasonal flowers in soft colors ranging from beige to peach, as well as white and blush. Touches of complementary and discreet foliage.*				
GROOM AND WITNESS'S BOUTONNIERES *Small jeweled boutonnieres that match the delicate flowers of the bride's bouquet*				
CEREMONY: FLORAL ARCH AND FLOWERS TO COVER THE AREA WHERE THE VOWS WILL BE EXCHANGED *Floral decor throughout the small stairways leading to the garden, including: flowers in planters, stairways, abundant floral arch*				
GROUND GARDEN FOR TABLE OF HONOR *Flower arrangement in the form of a ground garden, in soft colors ranging from beige to pink, and including white and blush, arranged on the ground at the head of the table of honor; approximately 30 in. (75 cm) long. Romantic and natural style, arrangement features abundant foliage and flowers.*				
DINNER: CENTERPIECES *Large arrangements, approximately 14 in. (35 cm) in diameter, done in a deconstructed style and placed on a small porcelain pedestal. Selection of seasonal flowers in soft colors. Container rental included.*				
DELIVERY, INSTALLATION, BREAKDOWN, *two people*				

TOTAL BEFORE TAXES	
TAX	
ALL TAXES INCLUDED	

Valid term for quote
Payment terms
Authorized for approval, date, and signature:

Legal Note to the Client: *It is important to familiarize yourself with the terms that are supplied with your quote.*

SAMPLE QUOTE

Trust is key for a quote to be accepted, and in order to trust you, your client needs to feel like you trust yourself. Before sending a quote, be sure to establish excellent communication from the start and build a mutually empathetic relationship.

I recommend that you don't send your quote just digitally. Make it your practice to request a telephone or in-person meeting where you can describe your proposal. If a meeting is not possible, take the time to write a precise explanatory email that clearly lays out your overall plans.

Pricing

Regardless of the premises, my quotes include three different types of pricing:

- floral pieces;
- installation and breakdown logistics;
- delivery.

Some florists build the "logistics" line item into each of the floral pieces; it varies from person to person. I myself prefer to separate it from the rest and clearly explain it to the client, because I believe it's important to value this part of our work, which is often substantial.

Let's break down these three components of the pricing.

- Floral pieces: There are two main techniques for determining the cost of this line item. The first one, which is most common at florists, consists of choosing a multiplier and applying it to the cost of the raw materials. This multiplier often varies between 2.5 and 4, depending on the florist. Your reputation and market position, as well as the amount of your costs, will allow you to determine that number. The second technique involves adding up the cost of your raw materials (plants and materials) and labor (work time needed to create your floral piece) and applying a margin of your choosing.

- Installation and breakdown: This is an important line item that should not be forgotten. It includes the following costs: wrapping your floral pieces, loading the truck, travel to the event location, unloading the truck on-site, installing each floral piece, breakdown time, travel, reloading and unloading the truck, and doing a studio reset when you return. Here, too, there are several schools of thought: you can, for example, determine a time for completing each of these tasks and multiply it by the hourly rate of your staff (or your own rate if you are working alone), or you can apply a percentage to the total cost of your floral pieces under this line item.

- Delivery: This line item includes the cost of renting a vehicle, if needed, as well as the cost of gas. If you use your own truck, you can also determine a cost per mile (kilometer), which will cover the fuel used and the maintenance costs for your vehicle.

A Meticulous Presentation

Beyond the calculations, there are tricks to presenting a quote so that it comes across as less severe, and to helping your client get accustomed to the process as you negotiate rates.

- I am careful to provide a nice description of each floral item on the quote itself. Rather than simply writing "Bride's bouquet," I write "Abundant, delicate, and romantic bride's bouquet, composed of seasonal flowers in autumnal colors ranging from burgundy to russet."

- I systematically attach a mood board to my quotes. It's a choice I have made from the start of my journey with Nebbia Studio. I am aware that this step represents time that will not necessarily be compensated if the client decides to work with another florist. However, I have been able to see that by providing visual bases from the start, the discussions are simpler and more fluid, and it is actually easier to convince the client that you are *the* person for their project. This first mood board is generally less detailed than the one used later as a work support once the project has begun.

- During the discussions, I am sure to never make my client feel uncomfortable about their budget, and I always try to find solutions. If, for example, they want to add a large floral suspension to the project, and the sample pictures they show me would cost well above what their budget allows, I would gently try to explain this to them by saying: "Oh yes, that hanging feature really packs a visual punch! For your project, I can offer you a version that is just as lovely and romantic, while maximizing the budget. We could use standard flowers in the same delicate colors as the ones in your example and rework the proportions." This way, instead of feeling frustrated, the client will see that you want to make them a tailored proposal that matches their wants and needs.

Negotiation Tips

After you send your quote, a client who wants to start negotiating will most probably respond with an offer to sign, provided you give them a reduction of however many dollars off the proposed amount.

An initial reaction, assuming you want to work on this project, might be to shave a bit off each line item. Perhaps take off 10 dollars here, 30 dollars there, to get down to the desired amount.

Let's take the example of a client who wants to reduce the quote for decorative flowers for his or her wedding by $550. If I change the ten floor arrangements that were planned for the ground garden in front of the bench from $110 to $55, explaining, however, that they will be smaller, my client will save $550. Bingo, quote signed!

Yet, if we take a closer look at the situation, I have actually reduced my profit and kept exactly the same amount of work. Making ten floor arrangements at $55 takes me as much time as doing ten floor arrangements at $110! Is that really the best solution?

Another approach might be to optimize my worktime by eliminating line items to reduce the budget. So if someone asks me to reduce my quote by $550, I'll propose keeping only five floor arrangements and strategically placing them along the path so that the result is still just as elegant but contains fewer flowers.

Ordering and Prepping Flowers

GETTING YOUR ORDER RIGHT

I won't deny it, ordering is kind of a stressful step. It's *the* moment when you can't make a mistake and when the questions start swirling around in your head. Will I have enough flowers? Did I order the right color? Will the flowers have time to fully open? Will all the varieties I discussed with the clients be available? While I have several years of ordering experience under my belt, it's still always a tense moment. But I'll reassure you that you can feel more confident if your method is sound!

The very first thing I do when I order large quantities of flowers is divide my budget in two. The first part will be for my wholesaler, who delivers to me directly at the studio, and with whom I must place an order a week before the date of my installation. The other portion is reserved for direct purchases from local growers. Since they have less visibility about the quantities they can offer, I buy from them two or three days before the date of my installation. The above distribution is very personal. It's up to you to find the right balance with your different suppliers, and it will also depend on their work practices. I use an order chart, which you'll find on the next page, both to make the task easier for myself and to prevent sleepless nights. The next step consists of gathering all the information that will allow you to fill in this chart. Feel free to change and adapt it to best suit your project.

THE IMPORTANCE OF PACKAGING

Once an order has been placed, it's time to figure out how to package the plants! This step is even more important when the flowers are delivered to you without water, because in that case, every minute counts. Properly preparing them will allow you to work with beautiful, well-hydrated flowers when arranging. I recommend that you follow the procedure below before the flowers arrive at the studio, to avoid losing time. It's a plan that I meticulously follow before each installation. Check that your knives and pruning shears are clean and sharp, which is essential for making clean cuts.

1. Prepare all your buckets. It's important to really wash them well to prevent the growth of bacteria. I personally use a mixture of white vinegar and water and then thoroughly rinse each bucket before filling up one-third of the container with fresh, clean water.

2. Tidy up the studio so you can work under good conditions and determine where you are going to store the flowers that have come in before they are prepped and placed in water.

3. Prepare your four garbage cans: one for plants to be composted, one for recyclable plastic, one for paper, and one for other waste.

Once the flowers have been received and the quantities confirmed with the delivery driver, prepare each variety individually (see next chapter). Place the flowers in high buckets for tall stems and low buckets for short stems: this prevents the flowers from getting damaged.

When they are ready, place your flower-filled buckets in a cool place away from direct sunlight.

I leave the flowers alone for at least twenty-four hours in the buckets they were delivered in before beginning the installation. This period is necessary for them to rehydrate, open up, and recover from the shock of transport. However, be careful to accurately figure out how long it takes the flowers you have chosen to open—some will arrive quite closed and will need

The Main Stages of a Floral Design Project

YOUR LOGO

FLOWER ORDER FORM

PLACE FLOWERS TO BE DELIVERED
Nebbia Studio

EVENT LOCATION
Address

PROJECT NAME

DELIVERY TIME
Between 7:00 a.m. and 9:00 a.m.

CLIENT CONTACT
Name and telephone number

NAME AND CONTACT INFORMATION OF DELIVERY PERSON
Sylvain (XXX-XXX-XXXX)

PROJECT INSTALLATION DATE

BUDGET FOR PURCHASING FLOWERS
$1,485.00

No. of Pieces	Type of Piece	Flower Variety 1 No. of Stems	Flower Variety 2 No. of Stems	Flower Variety 3 No. of Stems	Flower Variety 4 No. of Stems	Flower Variety 5 No. of Stems	Flower Variety 6 No. of Stems	Flower Variety 7 No. of Stems
1	Sideboard bouquet	5	5	5	5	5	10	10
1	Floral arch	19	19	19	19	19	20	20
10	Bud vases	2	2	2	2	2	2	2
2	Centerpieces	4	4	4	4	4	4	4
6	Garlands	3	3	3	3	3	4	4
1	Floral arrangement, stairs	10	10	10	10	10	18	18

Total number of stems	80	80	80	80	80	100	100
Price per stem before taxes	$1.53	$2.29	$0.76	$1.53	$0.98	$3.60	$3.60
Price before taxes	$122.40	$183.20	$60.80	$122.40	$78.40	$360.00	$360.00
Total price before taxes	$1,287.20						

SAMPLE ORDER CHART

more than twenty-four hours to open. This is the case for lilies and amaryllis, for example, so be sure to take it into consideration!

THE EFFICIENCY OF THE SERVICE SHEET

On the day of the installation, I want the situation to be under control and for nothing to be left to chance. To achieve this, I adapted a work document that I used when I was working in audiovisual production: the service sheet.

For photo or film shoots, a member of the production team drafts a daily service sheet and sends it to all participants. It includes the practical information for the day: the addresses of the shoot locations, the telephone numbers and names of the team members, the order of the scenes to be shot, the meeting times, and the required equipment.

The service sheet I adapted for floral installations is pretty much the same. I share it with my clients so they'll know what the setup will look like, and with the members of my team, so that they can all perform their duties independently.

ESTABLISHING YOUR BASE CAMP

I touched on this subject in the site visit section: if you need to finish off or even create arrangements on-site, it is best to establish a base camp. That's an area where you'll put all your equipment and flowers, and that will allow you to work more comfortably. Try not to spread yourself too thin, and respect your limits so that you can be more efficient.

The location of this base camp must be easy to access and close to the areas where you'll be working. You need to have a water source close by, as well as a worktable.

Print out the service sheet and mood board and put them up somewhere in this work area. However, be sure to never leave any quotes or invoices from your suppliers lying around. That information concerns you and you alone!

At your base camp, always have a small relaxation corner with snacks, water, and coffee—anything that you or your crew might enjoy when energy flags. Installation days can be very intense! Before leaving your studio, make sure you have everything you need:

- Your toolbox, containing everything you'll need at the installation location

- Chargers and batteries for your electrical equipment (your phone, your computer, your drill), as well as an extension cord

- A first-aid kit in case of any problems

- A cleaning kit so that you leave the installation location clean: garbage pails (opt for those round, soft plastic canvas pop-up bins; they take up no space once folded up), garbage bags, brooms, dustpan, plastic tarp or covers to place beneath your work areas

The Main Stages of a Floral Design Project

YOUR LOGO

SERVICE SHEET

CLIENT CONTACT INFORMATION
Name and telephone number

LUNCH BREAK
I plan for sandwiches and bottled water. If there are any food intolerances, allergies, or dietary restrictions, please let me know in advance.

EVENT LOCATION
Address

PROJECT NAME

DRESS CODE
Plain dark jeans + black T-shirt

PREP LOCATION
Nebbia Studio

PROJECT INSTALLATION DATE

TIME	LOCATION	DESCRIPTION	TEAM	VISUAL REFERENCE / COMMENTS
7:00 a.m.	NEBBIA STUDIO	Load up truck	JUSTINE - NADINE - PAUL - LUCILLE	
8:00 a.m.	NEBBIA STUDIO	Departure	JUSTINE - NADINE - PAUL - LUCILLE	
8:30 a.m.	BRIDE'S HOUSE	Delivery of bouquet	JUSTINE - NADINE - PAUL - LUCILLE	
9:00 a.m.	NAME OF EVENT LOCATION	Access to location—Start of event	JUSTINE - NADINE - PAUL - LUCILLE - ISA - CLAIRE	
9:00–10:00 a.m.	NAME OF EVENT LOCATION	Unload truck	JUSTINE - NADINE - PAUL - LUCILLE - ISA - CLAIRE	No direct access to garden, need to park in front of location and carry materials to garden > See if possible to put the flowers someplace cool and shady upon arrival.
10:00 a.m.–12:00 p.m.	NAME OF EVENT LOCATION	Flowering of five hanging installations Meal under tent (one per table)	JUSTINE - NADINE - PAUL - LUCILLE - ISA - CLAIRE	Hanging installations will be attached by cables to the tent the night before. Can stand on the tables underneath to work at the right height.
12:00–12:30 p.m.	NAME OF EVENT LOCATION	LUNCH BREAK	JUSTINE - NADINE - PAUL - LUCILLE - ISA - CLAIRE	
12:30–2:30 p.m.	NAME OF EVENT LOCATION	Installation of the following areas: Entry/gift area/cocktail and lounge area/table runner	LUCIE - ISA - PAUL	Place vases and arrangements that were previously finished at the studio. For the table runner, wait until the wedding planning team has put on the tablecloths before installing.
12:30–3:30 p.m.	NAME OF EVENT LOCATION	Installation of the following areas: Ceremony/music pavilion/seating plan/peacock chairs for the meal	JUSTINE - CLAIRE - NADINE	Ground gardens to be built on-site.
2:30–3:30 p.m.	NAME OF EVENT LOCATION	Load up truck		
3:30 p.m.	NAME OF EVENT LOCATION	INSTALLATION FINISHED, CLEAR OUT FOR ARRIVAL OF GUESTS!		

TEAM MEMBER	NAME	TELEPHONE NUMBER	CALL TIME AND LOCATION
HEAD FLORIST	JUSTINE		7:00 a.m.—Nebbia Studio
FREELANCE FLORIST 1	CLAIRE		9:00 a.m.—Event location
FREELANCE FLORIST 2	LUCILLE		6:00 a.m.—Nebbia Studio
FREELANCE FLORIST 3	ISA		9:00 a.m.—Event location
FREELANCE FLORIST 4	NADINE		6:00 a.m.—Nebbia Studio
RUNNER	PAUL		6:00 a.m.—Nebbia studio

SAMPLE SERVICE SHEET

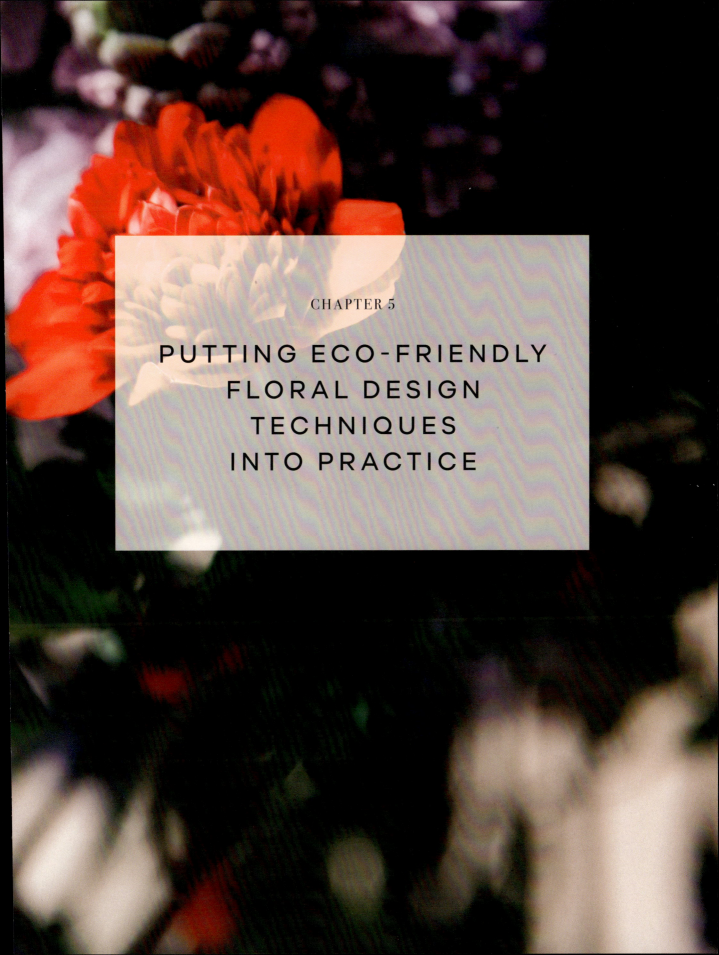

CHAPTER 5

PUTTING ECO-FRIENDLY FLORAL DESIGN TECHNIQUES INTO PRACTICE

Floral design involves expressing your creativity and carefully assembling the plants that you have so thoughtfully selected. In this section, I'll suggest some arranging techniques that I've implemented in my studio to limit my environmental footprint as much as possible. I learned these techniques on the job from fellow florists, in online forums, or in floristry textbooks.

These practices are not etched in stone. They're designed to evolve and improve through experience. I love to tell myself that the beauty of our profession also lies in our ability to challenge ourselves and grow! My goal is to reduce my use of floral foam in the arrangements I offer my clients as much as possible, to limit my use of single-use plastic, and to place recycling at the heart of the studio's business. In specific cases where floral foam is necessary for logistical reasons, I always choose the biodegradable products now available on the market.

Since the use of floral foam has already been extensively documented in training programs and other manuals, I'll focus here on all the lovely alternative techniques that are available to us! When I feel one of them could be improved, I'll tell you its limits and then you can experiment and reach your own opinion.

An Update on Absorbent Floral Foam

Green floral foam blocks arrived on the floristry scene in the 1960s. A minor technical revolution at the time, their use is very simple: when soaked in water and then inserted into a container or attached to a structure, they form a base into which flowers can easily be placed. Multiple types of flower arrangements can be created with them, and they're known for increasing durability, since they allow plants to be effectively hydrated. While they are a single-use product and must therefore be discarded after each use, they are inexpensive and thus don't have a large impact on the final price of the flower arrangement. All positive, you might say! Yet, the main problem with floral foam is actually the non-recyclable plastic contained within it. As waste, it forms minuscule particles as it breaks down, which pollute the land and wastewater, and can remain in the environment for hundreds of years. If we consider that thousands of tons of green foam have been used worldwide each year since it was invented, it's enough to make your head spin.

Floristry industry professionals are now becoming aware of the major environmental problem this material represents, and are increasingly deciding not to use it. You can find them on Instagram under hashtags such as #nofloralfoam and #floralfoamfree.

In addition to the techniques we'll discuss in this chapter, more ecological substitutes for green foam are arriving on the market. I'm thinking in particular of the Agra-Wool brand blocks made of basalt wool and sucrose, which I was able to test, or the OshunPouch plant-based pouches.

Putting Eco-Friendly Floral Design Techniques into Practice

Prepping Plants

Before you can start placing stems into your flower arrangements, you'll have to prepare and place your flowers into buckets. As discussed on page 80, this is a very important step of the preparation that will ensure the plants will last over time and open properly in the water. Once you have received your flowers, proceed as follows.

1 • Using your fingers, remove the leaves from the entire portion of the stem that will be immersed in the water. This will prevent bacteria from rapidly multiplying inside the bucket or vase.

2 • Next cut the stem diagonally at a 45-degree angle with a pruning knife or shears.

3 • Last, place the plant within a large amount of water, which you will ideally change every day, or every two days.

Some varieties of flowers require specific treatment to make them last.

- Bulbs, such as anemones, tulips, and ranunculus, prefer a straight cut of the stem and a container with little water. Tulips additionally have the annoying habit of drooping over the edge of the bucket. I recommend that you wrap them in newspaper in small groups of ten to keep them upright.

- Poppies, once cut, lose their precious sap and quickly wilt. It is therefore wise to burn the edge of their stems to seal up the cut. Once you have cut the poppies' stems, wait at least twenty-four hours before placing them in the same bucket as the other varieties, because their sap is aggressive.

- Woody plants such as lilacs or viburnum prefer to have their stems cut vertically 2 in. (5 cm) from their base.

RESULT AFTER CUTTING BULBS

87

- Hydrangeas like a high and long cut on the diagonal. You must be able to clearly see at least 2 in. (5 cm) of the white part inside the stem. I usually remove nearly all the stem's leaves so that the flower benefits from all the water it sucks up, and properly opens.

- Flowers such as carnations, which have knubby protrusions on their stems, must be cut below or above one of these nodes for the flowers to stay properly hydrated.

CARNATIONS AFTER BEING CUT

POPPIES AFTER BEING CUT

WOODY PLANTS AFTER BEING CUT

HYDRANGEAS AFTER BEING CUT

Delaying or Accelerating Blooming

Working with plants means you are working with living materials. The laws of nature dictate when they bloom, and their life cycle. Our job is nevertheless to offer nicely opened flowers that are bursting with health and freshness, on a given date. While we can't control those natural elements, there are methods that allow us to gain a bit of time or, conversely, slightly accelerate the natural process.

If you want to delay flowering, place flowers in a cool, dark environment (except in the case of tropical flowers, which don't like the cold). If, however, the goal is to make the flowers bloom a bit quicker, then place the bucket in a warm room with lots of light. You can also pour a bit of sugar into the water to boost their development.

Putting Eco-Friendly Floral Design Techniques into Practice

Types of Projects

BOUQUETS

Bouquets are most certainly the first floral arrangement one spontaneously attempts, starting in childhood. They're also the flower arrangements that allow us to convey our emotions. We offer them as a gift to say I love you, sorry, or thank you. In the hands of a bride, bouquets are the essential floral item of the day. Moreover, if there could be only a single item, bouquets would be it! As far as style, I love to make graphic, colorful bouquets, in deconstructed shapes. I use little to no greenery.

FLORAL ARRANGEMENTS

These medium-sized floral arrangements can serve several purposes. They can be centerpieces on a table, round out the decor on a photo shoot, or dress up an entryway. I'm offering you three techniques you can play around with, which rely on the use of adhesive tape, a kenzan, or a wire mesh structure. As far as the container goes, the possibilities are nearly infinite: from the most classic ceramic or glass vase to the boldest soup tureens or compote dishes, you can try any container that inspires you!

My Best Friend the Turntable!

Regardless of the technique used (adhesive tape, kenzan, or wire mesh), get in the habit of making your arrangements on a turntable. This will allow you to work in a full circle, efficiently and effortlessly. With a single move, you'll be able to get a complete view of your arrangement.

LARGE-SCALE FLORAL DECOR

These are by far my favorite pieces to make because you use your entire body to construct them. They allow you to decorate the biggest spaces and must be custom designed. Due to their size, these arrangements can be difficult to install at the event location. They sometimes present certain technical challenges, which you really need to think about in advance, particularly in the case of flower clouds, which need to be hung. They are majestic, intriguing, and impactful in absolutely any context. Wow factor guaranteed!

For these large floral arrangements, we'll use the chicken wire technique (see page 94). While the fundamentals are the same, the larger size of the arrangements introduces some technical issues that you shouldn't underestimate.

Get an Overview

Step back from time to time as you arrange to get a better idea of the end result.

BOUQUETS

The Spiral Bouquet

MATERIALS

- Pruning shears or florist knife
- Flowers
- Foliage (optional, if desired)
- Piece of string, 8 in. (20 cm)

Spiral bouquets are made using a traditional technique that yields a "clean" bouquet with well-aligned stems and a uniform overall structure. Flower stems are placed right next to one other while turning the whole bouquet around itself, producing its iconic shape. I make most bouquets other than brides' bouquets (page 95) by using this technique. It is built from the inside out, using both hands: the first hand is the "supporting hand," which will hold the bouquet together while the second hand, the "working hand," selects and places the flowers one by one. It's up to you to determine which hand will perform which task, so you can work comfortably!

I chose analogous colors with red (ranunculus, carnations), orange (ranunculus, poppies), and fuchsia (ranunculus, mini carnations, statices). To provide a bit of contrast, I used a touch of pale yellow (stock) and burgundy (scabiosa). This bouquet contains forty flowers.

PUTTING ECO-FRIENDLY FLORAL DESIGN TECHNIQUES INTO PRACTICE

Tip

To practice this technique, I recommend that you start by making small bouquets, like the one below. The more comfortable you feel with this exercise, the bigger you can make it. Your supporting hand needs to get used to firmly holding its grasp, and for a long time. It's not unusual for the hand holding the stems to hurt a bit, especially when you make one bouquet after another or create large pieces. Over time, your hand will get stronger, although you should be careful not to push too much!

1 • Using your fingers, pull off the leaves from the portion of stem that will be immersed in the water. This is the part underneath where you'll tie up the bouquet (where you'll place the string), and it should be clean and smooth. Place all the flowers in front of you on your worktable.

2 • Select two stems and make a cross in your supporting hand. Note that these first flowers will be at the center of your bouquet, because in a spiral bouquet, flowers are positioned around this central axis.

3 • Select a third stem and form a tripod of sorts.

91

STARTING YOUR FLORAL DESIGN STUDIO

4 • Place the next stem just alongside the third stem, maintaining a 45-degree angle. Continue in this way by placing the stems next to one another, always working in the same direction.

5 • Approximately every four or five flowers, turn the bouquet around: use your working hand to turn it, while the other hand continues to hold the bouquet at the point where you'll later tie it. This allows you to create new layers of stems. Your bouquet will slowly start to take shape.

6 • Once all the flowers are in your supporting hand, adjust the heights of the stems a little if necessary.

7 • Take a piece of string and press one end between the thumb of your supporting hand and the stems of your bouquet, at the narrowest point where it will be tied.

8 • Wrap the rest of the string around the bouquet, using your working hand, and knot both ends together.

9 • Cut all stems at the same point, on a 45-degree angle. If you have successfully formed your bouquet into a spiral shape, it will stand all by itself. Your bouquet will then be ready to be wrapped in a pretty piece of colored tissue paper. You can also add a colorful ribbon to bring out the colors of the flowers!

92

WHAT STYLE OF BOUQUET?

If you want to go for a deconstructed look, place some flowers a bit higher and others a bit lower than the general level. Conversely, if you want a compact, round effect, after each full turn in your hand, place the flowers a bit lower than the previous line.

ROUND BOUQUET

DECONSTRUCTED BOUQUET

BOUQUETS

Bouquets Using Wire Mesh

MATERIALS

- Green chicken wire
- Multipurpose shears
- Flowers
- Foliage (if desired)
- Piece of string, 8 in. (20 cm)
- Large mirror

The wire mesh technique consists of creating a base into which you can place flowers to stabilize them and give shape to the overall arrangement. This support allows you to obtain an ethereal, deconstructed look without cramming the flowers too close to one another. Once filled, the wire mesh base will remain invisible. The result is modern, and light-years away from the traditional round bouquet.

For this style of bouquet, I try to choose plants in different shapes and sizes, with many different textures. For example, in the bouquet shown here, the crepe-papery texture of the poppy contrasts with the velvetiness of the anemones, providing depth to the arrangement. As an aesthetic choice, I use very little greenery. I love to showcase the flowers and bring out their colors. This bouquet contains thirty-five individual flowers and features yellow ranunculus, beautiful purple anemones, salmon poppies, pale-yellow carnations, lilac stock, and salmon statice.

Putting Eco-Friendly Floral Design Techniques into Practice

Wedding Bouquets

I use the wire mesh technique primarily for brides' bouquets. I love to take my time to make these bouquets, which are so important for the ceremony. I start early in the calm of my studio, before my team arrives—it's almost a meditative moment for me! To ensure that it's fresh, I always make the bouquet the morning of the wedding. It's also extremely important to me to deliver the bouquet personally to the person who will carry it, and explain to them how to properly hold it. It's this tiny, very moving moment that is so special to me.

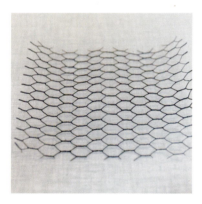

1 • Cut a 10 × 10 in. (25 × 25 cm) rectangle of wire mesh with your multipurpose shears, being careful to leave the sharp edges of the mesh on the outside.

2 • Roll the wire mesh into a cylinder and fold in the sharp edges so that everything is covered as desired.

3 • Tuck the ends in approximately 2 in. (5 cm) on each side.

4 • Prepare and clean the flowers and foliage as explained on page 87, trimming off any unsightly bits, such as damaged petals or excess leaves. Make sure that all the plants are ready before beginning to build your bouquet. This will enable you to concentrate fully on your arrangement. I usually keep only one flower per stem for this type of bouquet, which gives me greater control over the volume.

STARTING YOUR FLORAL DESIGN STUDIO

5 • Place the flowers in front of you on your workspace. I personally love to place each variety in its own vase to get a good overview of what I have available.

6 • Select a space in front of the mirror. Working in front of a mirror allows you to see the bouquet from the perspective of the guests (and the photographer!), which allows you full control over how it evolves and the final look.

7 • Take the wire mesh tube in your hand and start placing the first flowers, making sure to create different levels. I generally start with a few flowers of a single variety. Make sure that you place each flower through the first level of wire mesh, then the second, and so on, until you reach the spot where your hand is holding the bouquet.

8 • Add a second variety, creating the general shape you want for your bouquet. At this stage, the bouquet is still very unstable, but it will gradually become sturdier as you add flowers to it.

9 • Add the other flowers as well as the foliage.

10 • Once you have completed the bouquet, make sure that no wire mesh is visible. If you find some visible areas of mesh, place a very small flower there to hide the structure, while still not adding any additional volume to your arrangement.

96

Putting Eco-Friendly Floral Design Techniques into Practice

11 • Tie the stems of the bouquet at the thinnest part of the bouquet where all the stems meet, just above the hand that is holding the bouquet.

12 • Cut the stems straight across approximately 4 to 6 in. (10 to 15 cm) under the tie. Put the bouquet into a water-filled vase to store it until the client picks it up. If you want, add a colored ribbon right before you hand it to its recipient.

13 • Your bouquet is now complete and ready to be carefully wrapped for transport.

FLORAL ARRANGEMENTS

The Tape Grid

MATERIALS

- Adhesive tape (classic clear or special waterproof floral tape)
- Vase
- Flowers
- Greenery (if desired)
- Turntable (optional)

This technique is fairly basic, inexpensive, and within everyone's reach. It consists of building a grid pattern at the mouth of the vase, into which the flowers are then placed. Since the only materials needed are usually in everyone's drawer, it's very practical for making arrangements with a single type of flower or top-heavy flowers such as hydrangeas or peonies, or for marking out placement when using a vase with a strange or irregular shape. However, it requires using a significant amount of adhesive tape, which is a single-use, nonrecyclable material.

For this arrangement, I've used ivy leaves as my base, along with a few daffodil leaves. The ivy has tiny black berries that provide textural contrast against the flowers. I chose 'Fullstar' white anemones, blue mistral anemones, yellow ranunculus, yellow daffodils, and yellow carnations. This arrangement contains thirty-five flowers.

Putting Eco-Friendly Floral Design Techniques into Practice

1 • Fill the vase halfway with water. Make sure that the edges are completely dry. Cut strips of adhesive tape and place them on the vase, parallel to one another. If your arrangement mainly contains thin-stemmed flowers, space your strips approximately 0.75 in. (2 cm) apart. For thicker-stemmed flowers, such as amaryllis, leave 2 in. (5 cm) in between the strips.

2 • Turn your vase and repeat the same step in the other direction, so that you form a grid.

3 • Place a strip of tape around the rim of the base, making one complete turn to secure the grid. Your vase is now ready for your flowers.

4 • Prepare and clean the flowers and greenery according to the instructions on page 87, removing any unsightly bits, such as damaged petals or excess leaves.

5 • Start by placing the greenery.

6 • Place the flowers one by one. If you are using a turntable, turn your arrangement 360 degrees so that you can make sure it looks good from every angle, and adjust the arrangement as needed. Otherwise, turn it with your hands. Your arrangement is now ready.

FLORAL ARRANGEMENTS

Kenzans

MATERIALS

- Kenzan
- Vase
- Florist paste
- Flowers
- Greenery (if desired)
- Turntable (optional)

Kenzans are famous for being used in *ikebana*, the Japanese art of floral design. Their spiky iron base is placed at the bottom of the vase and used as a secure support for the flowers, which, once positioned, stay put. Infinitely reusable, they are a very eco-friendly tool that I prefer over all others. Some florists add a layer of chicken wire on top of the vase to further reinforce the structure.

Here I've used burning bush as an accent. I love it in winter, because the plants keep their leaves and produce stems that provide lovely lines in arrangements. Just be careful of their long thorns! The small red berries are rose hips. As for the flowers, this arrangement features pink and coral ranunculus, blue mistral anemones, red and white 'Fullstar' anemones, and blue hyacinths. It contains around sixty stems.

Putting Eco-Friendly Floral Design Techniques into Practice

1 • Roll a piece of floral paste around the kenzan, leaving a bit of excess, and fold the extra portion underneath.

2 • Place the kenzan at the bottom of the vase and really press it against the bottom. Turn it slightly so that it sticks to the container. While turning the vase, check that it is properly attached, then fill halfway with water.

3 • Cut each stem to the length of your choice and gradually stick them into the kenzan, flower by flower, working from the outside in. The stems must be cut straight across (rather than at the normal 45-degree angle) for them to stand properly between the metal spikes.

4 • The order in which you place your flowers depends on what style you want to achieve. For a minimalist arrangement, start with the focal flowers. If you're looking for a more abundant style, begin with the heaviest elements (branches, fruits, etc.), then add foliage to establish the general shape of the arrangement, finishing with the flowers.

5 • Turn your arrangement one full rotation on the turntable to ensure it looks good from every angle, and adjust as necessary. Your arrangement is now ready.

101

FLORAL ARRANGEMENTS

Wire Mesh Structure

MATERIALS

- Chicken wire
- Vase
- Adhesive tape (classic clear or special waterproof floral tape) or raffia
- Ruler or tape measure
- Flowers
- Greenery (if desired)
- Turntable (optional)

An alternative to the two preceding techniques, wire mesh's use extends well beyond this simple context. If you strive to work without floral foam, chicken wire will become your best friend. Nevertheless, before you try it out on other projects, get familiar with this technique by making some medium-size arrangements (like the one above).

Here I've swapped out the foliage for mimosa and statice, which I've used as filler flowers to maintain the monochromatic yellow look. These two flowers form a base while providing a textural contrast between the downy softness of the tiny mimosa flowers and the coarser look of the statice. Surrounding these two varieties are the other flowers I selected, all in different shades of yellow: poppies, ranunculus, tulips, and stock. 'Fullstar' anemones provide small pops of white. This arrangement contains approximately sixty stems.

Putting Eco-Friendly Floral Design Techniques into Practice

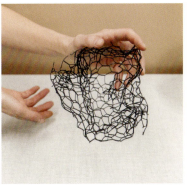

1 • Measure the opening of your vase to calculate how much mesh is needed. Double this measurement. Transpose the determined size onto your mesh and cut a square with the proper dimensions.

2 • Fold in two of the opposite sides to form a cylinder and close it up, folding in the opposite ends.

3 • Fold in the two remaining sides to form a makeshift ball with several layers to it. These layers will allow the flowers to get nestled into place and stand upright. Place the ball inside your vase and fill it with water.

4 • To secure the whole structure, place two pieces of adhesive tape in a cross shape on either end of the container or, for a more eco-friendly version, use raffia.

5 • Make your arrangement, putting in the filler flowers or greenery first, followed by the flowers, one by one. The first stems you place in might seem unstable, but as you gradually add more flowers, the structure will become more secure.

6 • Turn your arrangement one full rotation to make sure that it looks good from every angle, and adjust as necessary. Your arrangement is now ready.

LARGE-SCALE FLORAL DECOR

Floral Arrangement in an Oversized Vase

MATERIALS

- Chicken wire
- Decorative vase for the arrangement
- Plastic bucket appropriately sized for the vase
- Multipurpose shears
- Adhesive floral tape or reinforced raffia
- Flowers
- Greenery

Extra-large arrangements are often placed on pedestals, pillars, or other high architectural elements (along the banister or in an alcove). Having them perched that way makes them look even more impressive and majestic. I usually make these large-scale arrangements in lightweight plastic buckets and then place them in their vase. That way, I'm sure the container won't leak. Choose deep buckets at least 16 in. (40 cm) high to be sure that the tallest flowers stay upright.

I love to play with positive and negative space, highlighting the details. Here, this technique showcases large branches of rose hip and burning bush. My selection of flowers includes hyacinths, stock, and statice, along with blue anemones, ranunculus, carnations, and red 'Fullstar' anemones. This arrangement contains approximately 150 stems.

Putting Eco-Friendly Floral Design Techniques into Practice

1 • Check that the size of the bucket is appropriate for the vase. You can cut it down if necessary.

2 • Measure the width of the bucket and, using your shears, cut a square of chicken wire that is twice as wide as the bucket width. Form the chicken wire into a ball. Place a brick, stones, or other heavy item inside to weigh down your container.

3 • Place your chicken wire ball inside the bucket and attach it with adhesive tape, or with reinforced raffia (to avoid using plastic).

4 • Prepare and clean the flowers and foliage according to the instructions on page 87, removing any unsightly bits, such as a damaged petal or excessive leaves.

5 • Insert the foliage and a few flowers into the chicken wire, roughly shaping your arrangement. The more flowers you add, the more stable the structure will be. Make sure to turn your arrangement regularly to get a complete view.

6 • Add the flowers. If some flowers are too short to reach the water, put them in water tubes and place them in the foliage rather than directly in the wire. Turn your arrangement to make sure there are no holes and adjust as needed. Your arrangement is now ready.

LARGE-SCALE FLORAL DECOR

Grounded Arrangement

MATERIALS

- Chicken wire
- Long planter-type container
- Multipurpose shears
- Hot-glue gun
- Adhesive floral tape or reinforced raffia
- Flowers
- Greenery

Grounded flower arrangements are designed to be placed on the floor. These "ground gardens" can be used as a base in numerous situations. Placed end to end, they form a lovely, flowered alley. They can also be placed individually at the foot of a table or inside a fireplace. When added to each step of a flight of stairs, they make for a magnificent floral descent.

In this arrangement, I played with different heights to add a bit of movement to the whole. Therefore, the flowers at the front are intentionally low, while those at the back are higher. The analogous color palette ranges from pink to red, using orange poppies, ranunculus, and carnations along the way. The statice adds a few little pops of purple. This arrangement contains approximately eighty-five stems.

Putting Eco-Friendly Floral Design Techniques into Practice

1 • If you are using a planter, plug the little drainage holes with hot glue (you may be able to achieve a more eco-friendly method using secured pebbles) to make it waterproof. Then weigh it down with a brick, stones, or any other heavy item to make it stable.

2 • Measure the height of the container and, using shears, cut out a square of chicken wire that is five times as high as your container.

3 • Make a tube by rolling up one of the longer sides into the center of the rectangle. Do the same with the other side so that you have two tubes of wire that meet in the middle.

4 • Insert the shaped wire into the planter.

5 • Attach the chicken wire to at least four points along the length of the planter, using adhesive tape, or reinforced raffia if you want to avoid using plastic, and fill it with water.

6 • Prepare and clean the flowers and foliage as explained on page 87, removing any unsightly bits, such as damaged petals or excess leaves.

7 • Insert the greenery to form the base of your structure. Be sure that it covers up the planter.

8 • Place the flowers in the planter. Check that the flowers fully cover the planter. The flowers (not the container) should draw the attention. Your arrangement is now ready.

107

LARGE-SCALE FLORAL DECOR

Floral Pillars

MATERIALS

- Pillar structures
- Chicken wire
- Plastic containers
- Water tubes, clamp ring, wire, or hook-and-loop tape
- Flowers
- Sturdy greenery that holds up out of water
- Sandbags or cinder blocks (if needed)

This decorative floral element packs a visual punch. Whether you cover the entire surface with plants or opt for a more pared-down look, to be completely secure, pillars must be made the day of, on-site, and on solid, stable structures.

I've used long burning-bush branches and have added mimosa for heft. The latter is a good friend to large-scale installations, because a single branch provides a lot of volume. You therefore need very little to fill the decor. Nevertheless, these flowers dry up very quickly, and while it's possible to switch out dry branches from time to time during a shoot, you don't have this option with events. The rest of the yellow flowers are poppies, ranunculus, tulips, and stock. 'Fullstar' anemones provide pops of white. This piece contains nearly two hundred stems and four large mimosa bouquets.

Putting Eco-Friendly Floral Design Techniques into Practice

1 • Position your pillars, making sure that they are properly weighted: place sandbags or cinder blocks at the foot of the pillars. If the columns are located nearby an architectural element that you can connect to, fasten a cable to it so that it is more secure.

2 • Wrap your structure in several layers of chicken wire, creating thick masses and attaching them. I would always use cable ties, which are quick and easy to put in place but not reusable. Therefore, I now opt for wire or pieces of hook-and-loop tape.

3 • Determine which areas will have flowers that need water. Attach plastic containers there, making holes in the chicken wire, and then fill them with water.

4 • Now attach the branches of greenery to the structure.

5 • Prepare and clean the flowers and greenery according to the instructions on page 87, removing any unsightly bits, such as a damaged petal or excess leaves.

6 • Place the rest of the foliage and filler flowers (in this case, the mimosa), making sure to cover the entire structure.

7 • Place the flowers into the containers. Place the flowers that were previously inserted into the water tubes in their respective locations. Check that the containers are not visible, and conceal them with foliage if necessary.

8 • Spray water onto the foliage to refresh. Your arrangement is now ready.

Pillars

My pillars consist of two metal feet, 55 lbs. (25 kg) each, custom-made by a metalsmith, into which I inserted two wooden posts. I attached the longest branches to these two posts, enabling me to gain some height, but also achieve a more natural shape. I opted for a shape that looks a bit like an irregular arch as the structure for my arrangement.

You can find iron structures in more classic shapes at specialized stores. The flowering technique presented here can also be adapted for arches.

LARGE-SCALE FLORAL DECOR

Flower Clouds

MATERIALS

- Wooden rod, 36 in. (90 cm) long
- Chicken wire
- Floral wire
- Cable tie or hook-and-loop tape
- Metal wire and flat fastener
- Water tubes
- Flowers
- Foliage that lasts well without water
- Drill

A flower cloud is a flower arrangement that is suspended from the end of a cable or clear line. You can place it above a table during an event, in the background in the decor of a set, in the window of a boutique, and so on.

For flower clouds, I like to alternate between areas that contain a lot of flowers and those that contain fewer. This allows me to visually lighten the arrangement and create a pretty silhouette. I also often choose to insert certain flowers that are proportionately larger than the others in order to draw attention to a specific location. In this case, I had one particularly large poppy, which I placed at the bottom left. This is one of the first elements to which the eye goes when viewing the arrangement. I used approximately one hundred flowers to create this piece.

Safety First

Thoroughly check that the structure onto which you are fastening your floral installation is sturdy and reliable. It is preferable that the piece be created at the location where it will be displayed. In addition to transportation issues due to its size, it just makes it easier for you to work seamlessly and properly manage the arrangement's proportions.

Since they are often placed high, it is not rare for the part located above the composition to be completely invisible to viewers. Therefore, focus on the front, bottom, and back of the arrangement. Don't waste flowers trying to fill an area that no one will see.

1 • Drill a hole into each end of the wooden rod. Feed the metal wire through the holes, hang the structure from its support, and close up the wire again with the flat fastener.

2 • Cut off a piece of chicken wire that is the same width as your wooden rod and 32 in. (80 cm) long.

3 • Roll the rectangle of chicken wire around the wood to create a cylinder and attach it at several points with the floral wire. Close up the ends of the cylinder by folding the chicken wire up onto the wood and securing it with floral wire.

Putting Eco-Friendly Floral Design Techniques into Practice

4 • Prepare and clean the flowers and foliage according to the instructions on page 87, removing any unsightly bits, such as a damaged petal or excess leaves.

5 • Attach the branches of greenery to the structure, using floral wire, cable ties, or hook-and-loop tape, feeding it through the chicken wire at various points. Use the foliage to create the desired shape of the arrangement.

Secure Your Leaves

Once all the foliage has been attached, check that everything is secure. If certain stems seem loose to you, use your floral wire to attach them to each other or to the chicken wire.

6 • Add flowers in water tubes, making sure to always place them slightly tilted upward so that they don't spill. Generously spray water on the entire piece. Your arrangement is now ready.

Packaging and Transport

Most projects will be for events at a specific location. Transport and delivery are therefore part of the job. To avoid damaging pieces en route, you need to have some tricks up your sleeve.

BOUQUETS

If it's not for an event, a classic bouquet should be carefully wrapped in the colored paper of your choosing before delivering it to its recipient. This allows the flowers to be protected during transport. For environmental and aesthetic reasons, I never use plastic wrap.

For a bride's bouquet, you should devote the utmost attention to packaging, in order to avoid damage during delivery. I recommend that you use a square paper bag with a base measuring approximately 10 × 10 in. (25 × 25 cm) and create a little nest inside with tissue paper.

Place a glass with a little water in it in the center of your nest, then add the flowers. If possible, place the bouquet alongside you, beneath the passenger seat, so you can keep an eye on it during transport.

FLOWER ARRANGEMENTS

Arrangements made with floral foam are undeniably easier to transport than ones made using these eco-friendly techniques. From a strictly logistical point of view, foam has the benefit of keeping the water in when the arrangement is moving. Here is my technique to ensure the flowers are safely transported, with a minimum of water spilling. You'll need a crate that is slightly bigger than your floral arrangement, a protective cloth that is slightly larger than your box, some old cloths, terry cloth towels, and a squeeze bottle.

A BOUQUET IN ITS NEST

Putting Eco-Friendly Floral Design Techniques into Practice

1 • Make a little nest in the crate with your pieces of cloth and towels. The top of this nest should match the top of the vase so that it's snug. Place a protective cloth that is slightly larger than your crate on top.

2 • Place your flower arrangement inside the nest, on top of the protective cloth. Transport your arrangement, keeping the crate as straight as possible.

3 • At your installation site, remove the arrangement from the crate, pressing in both sides of the protective cloth. Wipe down the vase if any water spilled, and refill it by using the squeeze bottle.

LARGE-SCALE FLORAL DECOR

Large-scale flower arrangements travel poorly, which is why I strongly recommend that you assemble them on-site. If, however, timing reasons require you to work at the studio and transport them later, it is best to complete all the steps up to putting in the foliage, and not to add the flowers until you are at the installation site. Flowers do not tolerate transport well once they are in these large arrangements, because it is almost impossible to protect them as effectively as a small arrangement or bouquet.

When transporting oversized vase or grounded arrangements, first empty a bit of water from the container. They will be lighter, which will make your job easier. However, don't forget to quickly refill them once you reach your destination!

Don't hesitate to use a cord or string to secure arrangements in your vehicle and keep them from shifting during transport. And remember to have a dolly on hand, so you can move these hefty pieces without hurting yourself.

CHAPTER 6

WORKING ON YOUR COMMUNICATION SKILLS

When you launch a business, and especially in creative professions like ours, good communication is essential. It's what allows you to find clients, make a name for yourself, and expand your network.

The very first step is to define your visual identity. This contributes to building your brand and introducing it to the greatest number of people. This includes your business logo as well as a portfolio showing projects that best represent your work.

Once you've clearly defined these two aspects, you'll need to decide which communication methods you'll use to disseminate information. Whether they are digital or more traditional (flyers, brochures, business cards), there is no shortage of advertising methods. In this chapter, I'll cover only digital communication methods, and in particular the ones I use daily: my website, Instagram, and LinkedIn.

Naming Your Brand

Well now . . . have you already found your name? I hope so for your sake, because I would be truly incapable of advising you on this point; that's how much of a puzzle it was for me! I still sometimes randomly find absurd lists of proposed names written on the covers of magazines, on the corners of telephone bills, or even in draft emails. I racked my brain for a name for two years . . . two years! That might be a world record! I have pages and pages of names that I was unable to make my own.

Then one day, while I was riding my bike along a path, it all became clear. I was living in Milan at the time, working for a floral design studio on the other side of the city. I had just told my boss I was leaving to go back and live in France. I knew it was almost time to launch my business, even if the precise details of that project were still a little vague. It was a damp fall morning, and as I pedaled along, I felt good and savored the moment, one of the last in a city I loved so much. There was a thick fog, as there often is in Milan in October. How pretty it was, that fog, *la nebbia! La nebbia?*

Strangely, once I'd found the name of my business, everything quickly slid into place. It was as if that was the last obstacle I had to overcome!

Working On Your Communication Skills

Your Visual Identity

Whether you choose to feature a floral design style that is natural, baroque, sophisticated, contemporary, or minimalist, you'll need to think of the graphic elements that will accompany your flowers to strengthen your business's identity. The logo, the font or fonts, the colors—that's what we call visual identity.

Unless you were a graphic designer before getting into the flower business, I strongly recommend that you hire a professional to help create your visual identity. It's too important an aspect to be cobbled together. Don't necessarily look for a graphic designer who has already worked with florists. Instead, find someone who can faithfully reflect your vision, and who shows you a portfolio that speaks to you.

A corporate identity and style guide will enable you to have all visual elements of your brand in a single document: logo, icons, lettering, color chart . . . along with the context in which they will be used. It's a true graphic operating manual that allows you to communicate while maintaining a clear and consistent image across all your communication methods. If you hire an outside person to work on those areas of your business, such as a media consultant or web developer, a corporate identity and style guide will allow them to stick to the guidelines you've set in the visual aids.

To create Nebbia Studio's visual identity, I chose to work with Romain Chirat from the graphic design firm Établissements. Romain had already helped some of my friends and colleagues, and I adore his artistic sensibility. Regardless of the industry, he is always able to elegantly convey the essence of each of his clients.

THE VISUAL IDENTITY OF NEBBIA STUDIO
CREATED BY ÉTABLISSEMENTS

LOGO

Your logo stands for your business and sets you apart from the competition. It must represent your identity, and be easy to recognize and remember. You must be comfortable with its design and love it so much that you want to see it everywhere. Which will happen, by the way! Your logo will appear on all your communication methods: brochures, business cards, swag, website, the paper you use to wrap your bouquets . . .

Logo or Illustration?

Don't confuse logos with illustrations. A logo has a simple, minimalist design, while an illustration tells a story and contains a lot of stylistic details. A successful logo is easy to remember, adaptable to every format, and timeless, and it never goes out of fashion.

119

In our business sector, plant elements have pride of place on numerous logos. Yet, while it's clearly a good way to indicate the nature of our business to clients, it's certainly not a requirement.

I personally wanted a neutral, simple logo. I saw it as a stamp that would come to mark my floral arrangements.

My floral design features a very colorful, abundant style, so I wanted a logo that could visually tame that explosion of color. Of the three proposals Romain gave me, I chose the second one.

PROPOSED NEBBIA STUDIO LOGOS

LOGO SELECTED

COLORS

The same principles as those discussed on pages 64–67 apply here. Using the color wheel can definitely help you decide which colors best represent your brand.

Far from being insignificant, the colors that compose your visual identity will allow you create your entire aesthetic—and a thoughtfully constructed color palette will make it easier to identify your brand.

What Colors Symbolize

Here are a few examples of color perceptions:

- Red: passion, power, vigor
- Orange: vitality, pleasure, ambition
- Yellow: light, optimism, creativity
- Green: well-being, hope, growth
- Blue: wisdom, responsibility, reliability
- Purple: wisdom, spirituality, mystery
- Pink: sweetness, protection, romance
- Brown: authenticity, durability, simplicity
- White: simplicity, purity, innocence
- Black: elegance, modernity, sophistication
- Gray: neutrality, simplicity, sweetness

If you want to delve deeper into this fascinating subject, I recommend that you also read the works of color specialist and historian Michel Pastoureau.

When choosing these colors, you might consider the conventions of your business sector (florists very often choose green as the main color) or dare to use bold palettes to differentiate yourself.

Color symbolism should also be considered when determining your own palette. Indeed, every shade evokes emotion in the collective imagination, and color associations will have an impact on how your visual identity will be perceived. This appreciation of color is very culturally entrenched. In color specialist Jean-Gabriel Causse's book *L'Étonnant Pouvoir des Couleurs* (The Surprising Power of Colors), he provides a perfect example of the symbolic differences across different geographic regions of the world.

In Japan, for example, blue evokes malice and ill will, while in China the same color evokes wisdom and immortality. Color can also have different meanings depending on its field of application. In this same book, Causse brings up the issue of red on packaging. He explains that red symbolizes love or passion on perfume packaging, while on packaging for mass consumer products it evokes "a good deal, since it's not expensive," and will be used to try to get people to make impulse buys.

FONT

The font allows all letters of the alphabet, numbers, and special characters to be transcribed. The font chosen to write your texts forms an integral part of your visual identity, just like the logo and colors you choose. Whether used in a tagline beneath your logo, or on your communications or other business documents (like quotes or invoices), it should be chosen with care.

There are four categories of fonts.

- Serif fonts: Fonts with a serif (a projection finishing off the stroke of a letter). They are classic and traditional. They provide a high-end look and add an important, serious feel to the message being read.

Serif Fonts

- Sans serif fonts: Fonts with no projection on the finishing strokes of the letters. Since these fonts are easier to read and the plainest, they are often recommended when there is lots of content. They lend a modern and creative feel to the message being read.

Sans Serif Fonts

- Script fonts: Fonts with a handwritten or calligraphy look. They provide an elegant and romantic feel to the message. They are aesthetically pleasing. Since they are less legible than the others, it's better to avoid using them for long texts.

Script Fonts

- Display or decorative fonts: Attractive and original, these fonts provide a strong visual impact. They are generally used to transcribe a title or a very short text.

DISPLAY FONTS

DEFINE YOUR VISUAL IDENTITY

A brand's visual identity allows you to use non-verbal tools to convey a message, and to build an aesthetic that simultaneously fits what you are offering and your values. These latter aspects are what will guide you in choosing your logo, colors, fonts, etc.

To determine what would best represent your brand, start by thinking about your business. To do so, I suggest that you follow a five-step process.

1. Describe your work, using a few simple words that explain what you do and your core business.

2. List the values your business embraces, and explain why they are important to you.

3. Identify what makes your business unique.

4. Analyze the visual identities of your competitors (logos, colors, fonts) and think about what you like and don't like.

5. Make a Pinterest board with the logos and visual identities of different kinds of brands that you like. Try to understand why you like them, and figure out what characteristics they have in common.

You can provide your graphic designer with all the information you have gathered. It will help them to effectively assist you as you build your visual identity.

EXPERT ADVICE

Romain Chirat, art director and graphic designer at Établissements Studio

Romain founded Établissements Studio, a graphic design and art direction studio that specializes in visual identity.
His know-how extends to every medium imaginable for enhancing a product or brand.
Here is Romain's advice for creating a successful visual identity.

- First, choose your graphic designer or art director wisely: it's better to select someone who shares the same sensibilities. It is always a waste of time (and money) to force a creative person to work outside their aesthetic.

- Never give in to trendy effects; having a great visual identity is an investment for a young business. Therefore, you need to think long-term and bet on a logo that will stand the test of time.

- As time goes by, adapt your logo colors, so you can give it a fresh spin and avoid getting bored with it.

- Pay attention to packaging and client experience, which are both as important as the logo. Above all, be meticulous in your communication. Pay close attention to the quality of the photos you post online, and especially on social media. It's a window into your aesthetic vision and gives a sense of how serious you are, so don't neglect a single detail.

www.etablissements.studio
@etablissements.studio

Your Portfolio

When you first become a florist, you often start out working for other florists. Therefore, photos of the floral arrangements you've made don't belong to you, and you cannot use them in your communications.

When I founded Nebbia Studio, this was my situation. I had two years of experience in the business, but very few photos to show my future clients. I thus had to build my portfolio from scratch.

I recommend building a portfolio in two stages:

1. Organize a photo shoot to take pictures of representative arrangements you'll offer your future clients;

2. As your business evolves, select client projects that are best suited to defining your brand identity.

ORGANIZING YOUR FIRST SHOOT

The size of this shoot will depend on what you can invest financially. Yet, there's no need to create colossal projects. The important thing is to successfully convey your style so you can attract clients that are a good fit.

A series of arrangements placed on a pretty, textured pedestal in front of a colored background can start off your portfolio. When I launched my business, I chose three types of images: photos of arrangements in vases, photos of bouquets in my hands, because I wanted to stage myself with the arrangements, and portraits of flowers. To maintain a consistent look in the different types of photographs, I highlighted two colors: orange and blue.

PHOTOS TAKEN AT THE FIRST
NEBBIA STUDIO PHOTO SHOOT

Using this as my base, I began posting on social media sites, sending newsletters, and producing my first advertising materials (website, flyers, etc.).

Just as you would for a classic project for a client, organize yourself conscientiously: create an inspiration board on Pinterest, a color palette, a complete mood board; make sketches of your arrangements; and choose your flowers with precision. Plan your photo shoot carefully to obtain the best images to showcase your work. And make sure that your photos are of good quality. I can't overemphasize how important that point is. Your portfolio must be professional. If you yourself are not a good photographer, certainly there's someone in your circle of friends and family who would be thrilled to be a part of your project. There is nothing more frustrating than spending time designing and creating amazing floral arrangements and ending up with photos that are not up to snuff.

Also think about how to take advantage of your network. Do you want to launch a line of bouquets for subscription to professionals? You'll need photos of the arrangements in context. Perhaps that uncle of yours who opened a pretty boutique hotel would love to have you do a photo shoot with your flowers in the lobby in exchange for a few bouquets? And that friend who's working on her debut line of scented candles? You could join forces to create a superb setting that would serve both of your businesses.

If you want to get started in the world of weddings, know that there is an interesting solution for producing high-quality photos: inspiration shoots. The idea of these photo shoots is to bring together a group of industry professionals and pool their expertise: a photographer, a wedding planner, a cake designer, a wedding dress designer, a florist . . . each person showcases their know-how, and everyone leaves with beautiful pictures.

One Project, One Photo

Amid the frenzy of making bouquets or placing arrangements, taking great photos of your creations is often last on the to-do list. It's only when you go to add a project to your portfolio that you realize you don't have good-quality shots. So always set aside a few minutes to take pictures from different angles and immortalize your work. Note that only good-quality photos should be used in your portfolio or social media.

SELECTING IMAGES

After the first photo shoot, select the best shots to include in a slideshow. Add the name you assigned to your series if relevant.

Over time, you'll start accumulating an increasing number of representative projects and photos. Not every shot will have a place in your portfolio or communication materials. You'll need to learn to critique your work and really be able to analyze each image you post. In this visual and creative profession, sharing an image is not insignificant. In fact, your work opportunities will often be a direct result of this type of content.

When I choose the photos I post, I systematically ask myself two questions.

1. *Will I want to redo this same project?* Clients will often come to you with photos of your work that they found on your social media or website and ask you for something similar. So be sure to post photos only of floral pieces you are proud of and would like to reproduce!

2. *Does this photo really highlight the arrangement?* Taking a successful photo of a flower arrangement requires a certain degree of expertise. The camera angle and light should enhance your work. Also pay attention to filters, which can diminish the color palette of your flowers. If your arrangement is a lot less beautiful in the photo than in real life, then don't use that image.

Remember that no slapdash photo taken in a fit of panic will ever pass the quality control needed to be added to your portfolio or social media! If one of your projects is very important for your catalog, organize yourself in advance to make sure you get images that can be used. Once you have high-quality photos, make sure there is consistency across the group. Your various projects should work with one another. Finding visual unity is even more difficult when you work with a lot of different colors. Therefore, it might be interesting to arrange your photos by color range, even if they are from different projects.

Your Website

Having a good online presence has become essential for attracting and retaining a loyal clientele, especially if you are a studio florist with no physical point of sale. Your website might simply serve as a shop window, a place where your potential clients can go to see what you offer, and then contact you. Or it might be an e-commerce interface where they can make purchases. Regardless, it should faithfully represent the essence and quality of your work. When starting your business, a website is definitely one investment to consider.

CREATING YOUR WEBSITE

You have two options for creating your website. You can do it yourself or hire professionals to design it. What you decide depends on your own technical capabilities and your financial means.

When I created Nebbia Studio, I chose to do my website myself for the first year of business. The profit I had reaped by the end of that period allowed me to hire a professional the following year. Here are a few pieces of advice depending on your circumstances.

- **Design your website yourself:** If you choose to create your website on your own, there's no need to know how to code! There are now numerous solutions available to you that will allow you to create a clean, functional website. You'll need to first choose a domain name and register it with the extension of your choosing (.com, for example). You can register your domain name with a registrar, or registration office, or most simply, with your site's hosting service. There are numerous publishers available online at a variety of rates that allow you to create your website yourself. I did mine with Squarespace, since I liked the design and found it fairly easy to use. Consider using Shopify directly, if you are building an e-commerce site. All these sites offer templates with predesigned layouts for web pages. Whether they are paid services or free, they are often easy to use and customize with your information and photos.

- **Call on a professional:** If you choose to hire a professional to create your website, choose carefully. You can hire either a freelancer or a web agency. Site design requires particular expertise in several different aspects (design, development, search engine optimization, etc.), and a given freelancer often specializes in a very specific domain. It is quite rare to find someone who is excellent in every area, so really research your potential provider's profile before beginning your collaboration. As for a web agency, it will have all the internal resources and expertise needed to handle your site. A team with specialists from each area will manage the design. Yet, clearly an agency's fee will be much higher than a freelancer's.

In both cases, I recommend that you provide a list of specifications so that you can thoroughly articulate your needs. You can provide a precise description of your business, your website's objectives (for example, finding new clients, explaining your services, improving your visibility), examples of sites you like, and when you'll need your platform to be ready.

SITE ESSENTIALS

Whichever design option you choose, your site must contain the following basic elements to be functional and effective.

- Great photographs: As we have seen, it is essential to have great photos. They'll illustrate each page of your website according to its theme.

Working On Your Communication Skills

- Clear breakdown of your services: You need your clients to understand with a quick glance what you can do for them. Your services must be listed and defined. Highlight those you most want to develop.

- A clear indication of where you work and how far you'll travel: That's important, particularly for people who travel outside their city or region for set design projects or events. Clients sometimes don't realize the logistics that come with long travel times. If you are ready to travel the world to provide flowers, no problem. Otherwise, set clear limits. You don't want people contacting you about a wedding in Phoenix when your studio is in Boston!

- Introduce yourself: I know all too well how tough this can be for the more reserved among us. But it's nevertheless truly added value. Clients love to know the person they are doing business with, especially for a creative job where the provider's personality plays a large role. You don't need to tell them your whole life story! Just explain what led you to work in flowers, and talk about what you like about your business. They should be able to see that you are passionate about what you do and get a sense of your style.

- Your values: Your principles contribute to your brand's identity. Clients appreciate working with professionals who share their own values. To define your values, define your ideal client and your business's mission statement.

- Blogs: Having a blog allows you to provide new information on your website without having to actually update it. A blog attracts traffic and provides visibility.

- CTAs or calls to action: an essential marketing tool, the call-to-action button is a clickable element that invites the visitor to go further and complete a specific action on the platform. "Contact Us," "Subscribe," and "Share" are examples of this.

- Testimonials: These are a gauge of confidence in your services. For many consumers, reading the testimonials has become an automatic part of the purchasing process. There's no reason to publish dozens of them on your site, but I would say you need at least three to be credible.

- A mobile version: your website should be optimized to be used on a cell phone, since most internet users will be consulting it from their phones.

EXPERT ADVICE
Émilie Viala, specialized SEO web designer and digital strategy consultant at Marwee

Émilie is the founder of Marwee. Specializing in search engine optimization, digital strategy, and the creation of websites, she helps passionate craftspeople and designers boost their internet presence by creating a powerful, authentic form of communication.

Search engine optimization (or SEO) is one of the key elements for increasing your site's visibility. It allows you to optimize your site on search engines such as Google in an evolving, sustainable manner. Here are a few pieces of advice for successful SEO.

- Before designing your site, think about your content strategy. What are your site's objectives, what services do you want to showcase, what keywords do you want to be discovered, what words would attract your ideal clients... This will help you create pertinent, high-quality, and well-structured content going forward.

- Rank your content. In order to classify you, robots prioritize your various titles. Don't forget to add some and to develop them carefully, incorporating your preferred key words.

- Choose the right search term (or rather the lengthiest one). In fact, 69 percent of Google searches contain more than four words. You should therefore prioritize detailed keywords that meet your clients' needs. They will be a lot more competitive and will generate sales.

- Reduce the size of your images. Your site's technical performance is a cornerstone of SEO. So hunt down those super-large photo files in your library and optimize them without diminishing their quality.

There are dozens of other tips like this, but remember one thing: the algorithm is not the enemy, quite the opposite. It just wants to give a pertinent response to internet users' requests. It has neither feelings nor prejudices. If your website does not appear among the top results, it's because your content is not clear, powerful, or rich enough for the algorithm... or for the end reader. So optimize it!

www.marwee.fr
@marwee.fr

Social Media

The world of social media is quickly evolving. Managing it is time consuming and could be a full-time activity. If you are alone at the helm of your business, choose one or two platforms to be active on rather than scattering yourself too thin across every interface. In fact, it's important to be somewhat rigorous in your activities and post regularly so that the algorithms don't leave you behind. Carve out weekly blocks of time devoted to working on your content, planning out your posts, and attending to your numerous other duties.

There are a multitude of tools to help you manage social media, depending on the platform concerned. There are also online resources that allow you to understand the inner workings of the networks you have selected. For example, I'm thinking of platforms such as Domestika that offer subject-specific courses from industry professionals, which will allow you to stay current.

INSTAGRAM

Instagram is my preferred social media site. I can share what I'm passionate about and interact with my community. The key element for increasing visibility on it is posting regularly and interacting with followers. As I am writing this chapter, how we share content is evolving. Videos are favored over photos, which until recently were the heart and soul of Instagram. You therefore have to keep an eye on how networks evolve to be able to adapt and stay visible.

Here are six tips for managing your Instagram account.

1. Define your audience and its needs. For example, my main audience consists of flower lovers, which can then be divided into two subcategories: florists or aspiring florists, and people who are potentially interested in my services for a floral set design project.

2. Determine which types of content might attract your audience. I personally have defined five of them: work-in-progress or making-of videos of my floral set design projects, pretty photos of those finished projects, portraits of people with whom I collaborate (flower growers, ceramicists, and so on), advice on floral design, and resources (books or podcasts) that I find inspirational or helpful.

3. Post different types of content in all categories: each section should be specific. Under Stories, I post "imperfect" videos, shot spontaneously. This type of format works well for sharing my daily life at the studio (for example, a flower delivery, or the arrival of new containers). I use Reels for more finished videos, such as how-to videos or florist hacks. Most often, I post pretty photos of finished projects.

4. Pay attention to the captions on your posts and reels. They can tell a story or be very minimalist, and can prompt discussion or action.

5. Use good hashtags. Hashtags are the SEO of Instagram, so use them to increase your visibility. They must be specific to your business. Let's use the example of a florist from the Dallas region who creates content for Dallas residents. Incorporating the hashtag #dallas, which has twenty-four million publications, seems pretty useless. There is very little chance that your publication would find a place in that jungle! Conversely, the hashtag #dallasflorist has "only" 95,000 and is followed only by residents interested in flowers.

STARTING YOUR FLORAL DESIGN STUDIO

6. Planning how to manage social networks is very time consuming. To be efficient: plan what you'll post! There are very good tools for this, such as Planoly and Later. All these applications will allow you to make a publications calendar and view your grid (the Instagram photos grid).

LINKEDIN

LinkedIn is the professional world's main platform. It provides a digital dimension to classic networking, and also legitimizes your business. Likewise, it's a great tool for finding new clients and associates, or for taking stock of the industry. I'm less active on LinkedIn than on Instagram for time's sake, but I do make sure to regularly interact with my professional community and post content on my business page at least once or twice a month.

Here are a few basic tips for using LinkedIn.

- When you create your personal page, add as much information as possible. Write up a detailed bio and describe all your professional experience. Indicate your training, your expertise, and what languages you speak.

- Create a page for your business: Really differentiate your business page from your personal profile. Since a business cannot have a profile on LinkedIn, you need to create a distinct account. Indicate your work, your website's URL, the size of your company, and where it is located.

- Start networking: It's important to respect best practices on LinkedIn. It's pointless to chase followers—prioritize relationships you think will be pertinent and useful. Add people with whom you work as you meet them, and look for others with whom you share common professional interests.

- Pass along important information from your business sector that you see on other people's profiles, to create a flow of activity and discussion.

- Create posts to share news about your business: a special project, a publication in the press, a new product, or a new service.

132

EXPERT ADVICE

Simoné Eusebio, director of communications at Make My Lemonade

Simoné Eusebio is in charge of developing and enhancing brand image and establishing actions and strategies across all communications media at the brand Make My Lemonade. A social media expert, Simoné gives us three pieces of advice for successfully communicating on Instagram.

Be genuine rather than perfect

For some years now, Instagram has become something of a sterile platform, a very contrived window with professional images and very little spontaneous content. As you can see from the success of TikTok, users are drawn to more direct, less rehearsed content. Without completely abandoning aesthetics and your artistic direction, you can easily recount your daily life, using simple visual concepts, and create a connection with your community. The trend of the "dumb photo" really illustrates this evolution. It consists of posting a stream of natural, unedited photos. Tell your story; show your successes, and sometimes your failures too. Talk about what you believe and what you are unsure about. Provide content that draws people in and makes them want to know what will happen next, just like a good television series does!

The text is as important as the image

The social media frenzy has resulted in quick mass-consumed content. We tend to think of the text as unimportant—but that's false! Blogs, the predecessors to social networks, are there to remind us of it. In your story or feed, take the time to write, and even to write a lot sometimes! Your words will allow you to give users a reading break, to explain what an image can't show, and to create engagement. Not to mention that the search engines adore reading your texts for SEO purposes. So pick up your pens!

"Chi va piano va sano"

Respect the Italian proverb "Slow is safe"! Don't try to grow your community at all costs. Large-scale contests, for example, will win you followers who are interested only in profit. They will unsubscribe as soon as the contest has ended or will not pay attention to your other content. To expand your community, target groups of people through actions that have real added value. Post photos of the people you collaborate with, dream up educational content with partners in a given field, do a theme week centering on a particular project. These publications will be appreciated and shared because they were carefully thought out and genuine.

www.makemylemonade.com
@makemylemonade

CHAPTER 7

CASE STUDIES

STARTING YOUR FLORAL DESIGN STUDIO

Dutch Still Life with Iconographia

In this chapter, I'll introduce you to three of my projects. Reviewing the different stages of the process will allow you to specifically grasp how a floral designer's work is organized. I chose three very different types of clients to show the range of people with whom floral designers can work. These projects also showcase the most typical clients for my business: an art direction and photography studio, a brand, and a wedding and event planner.

THE CLIENT

Iconographia is a creative duo composed of Clémence, who is a photographer, and Armâne, an art director (to find them on the web, go to www.iconographia.fr, @studio.iconographia). With their multidisciplinary process centering on art history, and thanks to their painterly treatment of photography, these talented young women have built a strong, recognizable artistic identity.

Project after project, these fervent feminists question woman's place in art history, whether as artist or subject. In the past few years, they have won numerous photography prizes and participated in multiple exhibitions, particularly the prestigious Salon de la Société Nationale des Beaux-Arts.

Their clientele is quite eclectic. They work equally well with individuals and professionals, including musicians, wedding-dress designers, interior design brands, or jewelry houses. It so happens that I discovered their work while leafing through an excellent ad campaign. It was an homage to Art Nouveau done for the Maindelion jewelry house, which used the beautiful Adeline Rapon as their model. We did not know one another yet, but I meticulously saved their images on Instagram.

CLIENT BRIEF

Clémence and Armâne contacted me about a still-life project. They wanted to shake up their style a bit and work with a more colorful palette than they usually did, making fresh flowers their main subject. Our collaboration was part of a research project they called "Peintresses" ("Paintresses"). The goal was to pay homage or, rather, "femmage," as they prefer to put it, to the oft-forgotten work of major female artists throughout history, by reinterpreting their artwork. They proposed Dutch painter Rachel Ruysch (1664–1750) as the subject of this six-handed project.

Rachel Ruysch was part of the art movement known as "the golden age of Dutch painting." She is primarily known for her realistic still-life paintings. The daughter of a professor of botany, she assisted her father in preparing plants to be preserved. This gave her access to an exceptional range of materials. The fact that flowers became her preferred painting subject is therefore not surprising.

For this artistic project, I was instructed to make a medium-sized floral arrangement that would be placed in front of a textured painted background made by Armâne and Clémence. That decor would then be further enhanced by their lighting work and postproduction processing of the image.

Prior to our first discussion, the pair from Iconographia had done a mood board, which included pictures of flower arrangements from my portfolio and other designers' portfolios, as well as several Rachel Ruysch paintings. Based on this, I was able to understand what they wanted and needed after just a quick look.

A CREATIVE PROPOSAL

I had already worked in the past on a series of images inspired by the floral arrangements in Dutch still-life paintings. Yet, at the time, I'd decided to shake things up and create something with much more of a pop art feel. For that project, I'd chosen a very flashy color palette and used quirky accessories such as little colored soda bottles, magazines, books, and shells.

I had somewhat of a different vision for this collaboration with Iconographia. I wanted to stay rooted in their usual artistic process, and, in doing so, create something that faithfully reflected how Rachel Ruysch would have arranged flowers in the golden age of Dutch painting. Nevertheless, what's hard about this type of exercise is resisting the urge to just copy/paste the original subject.

PHOTOS FROM THE FIRST SERIES

PHOTOS FROM THE SECOND SERIES

The first stage of my process was to study the artist's paintings to determine their signature elements. In other words, the details that characterized her style, how she composed the flowers on the canvas.

The second stage consisted of sorting these elements and determining which ones to keep. I pinpointed six defining features of Rachel Ruysch's floral arrangements.

1. A wide selection of plant varieties.

2. Very open, sometimes even wilted flowers.

3. A mix of warm and cool colors.

4. Movement in all directions.

5. A vase/container with a very minimal visual presence.

6. High, oval-shaped arrangement.

The last point caught my attention because I tend to develop my arrangements in a V shape—that's my signature element. I of course also work with round or oval shapes, but those shapes are not what come to me instinctively.

I decided to implement the first five points à la Rachel Ruysch, and to handle the sixth as I would normally in my own arrangements.

CREATING THE ARRANGEMENTS

Flowers

For this project, it was very important to have a selection of flowers that were of high quality, but not all uniform. Rachel Ruysch's arrangements were made with very pretty flowers that seemed to have been plucked straight from her garden. So I had to find raw materials that were up to snuff. I chose to work with a flower farm to ensure that I had access to a wide range of plants that met these criteria.

Marlène, from Les Batisses flower farm, assisted me on this project. My shopping list was as follows: anemones, tulips, ranunculus, foxglove, lupines, sweet pea, bearded iris, alliums, heuchera, and veronica.

Arrangement Technique

I used ten different varieties of flowers, as was Rachel Ruysch's custom. They were all carefully selected for their aesthetic qualities, featuring lovely, complementary shapes and multiple textures. In total, I used approximately one hundred stems to make this arrangement.

There were five days between when I bought the flowers and the photo shoot. During that time, I stored the plants at room temperature, taking care to change the water every day so they continued to open. This allowed them to reach the perfect stage of maturity on the actual day of the shoot. Some of the flowers, such as the ranunculus, were so open that it would have been absolutely impossible for me to use them in a classic project requiring the freshest flowers.

STILL LIFE WITH FLOWERS,
RACHEL RUYSCH (1664-1750)

FLOWERS IN A GLASS VASE, 1704,
RACHEL RUYSCH

The color palette for the selected flowers was a mix of warm (red, yellow, orange, and burgundy) and cool (violet, lilac, and green) colors.

To create the arrangement, I used the chicken wire technique (see page 94). I could have also used the kenzan technique, but for a project of this size, I preferred a process that would further guarantee the stability of the plants. I made the arrangement in a very simple and discreet bowl, so that it would be nearly invisible.

Once I had set it up for the photo shoot, I then added flowers that completely defied the laws of gravity, as in Ruysch's paintings. To do so, I hung some of them on a metallic stem, which was then erased during postproduction. A little trick that you now know!

Time and Resources Needed

The timing of the whole project could be broken down as follows:

- two hours of research and analysis of the work of Rachel Ruysch—one person
- one hour for choosing flowers in the Batisse fields—one person
- two hours for cleaning and preparing plants—one person
- a little more than one hour to complete the arrangement on site at the Iconographia studio—one person

Making Your Composition Photogenic

The difficulty with this type of work is that each flower must be placed very precisely. Looking at something on-screen is very different that looking with your eye, since arrangements tend to look flatter in photos. During shoots, I like to see how the arrangement is evolving through the lens of the camera or on the feed. I often asked Clémence to take a few "in-process" shots so I could really get a sense of the volume and be able to make adjustments on the spot.

OVAL-SHAPED ARRANGEMENT

V-SHAPED ARRANGEMENT

Case Studies

The Event at the Make My Lemonade Boutique

THE CLIENT

Make My Lemonade is a ready-to-wear brand founded by designer Lisa Gachet (to find her on the web, go to www.makemylemonade.com, @makemylemonade). The adventure began in 2012 as a lifestyle and DIY blog through which Lisa would invite her readers to make things with their own two hands. Bolstered by its success, the blog quickly evolved into a brand of limited-edition clothing, which you could either make yourself or buy ready to wear. Make My Lemonade embodies a lighthearted, uninhibited, and happy-go-lucky style. Each of the many collections features strong colors and bold prints. Flowers are a constant, and are found on clothing fabric patterns, in the background of advertising campaigns, or as the subjects of numerous DIY projects. I have a very special relationship with the brand because Lisa and I are old friends.

When I was getting started in floral design, I did my very first collaborations with Make My Lemonade. It is always an enormous pleasure for me to participate in their projects. Each one is a creative mash-up that ventures deep into uncharted territory.

THE CLIENT BRIEF

The flowered car is now a classic at Make My Lemonade. The very first one was done to celebrate the boutique's opening. It was a magnificent yellow Alfa Romeo done up in flowers by the team from Pampa Paris. I did the second one, which served as a set for shooting the campaign for the "Flower Remedy" collection. On this project, I had chosen to work with analogous colors in shades of orange and pink. The goal was to create a uniform backdrop so that the clothing showed up well and people didn't pay attention only to the flowered car.

I'd like to go into a little more detail here about the third flowered car I did. I was assigned this project to lead the launch of Make My Lemonade's summer collection, "Paris to Memphis." The floral decor was supposed to draw passersby's attention and invite them to stop in at the boutique. The happy, colorful collection, filled with geometric prints, was an homage to the Memphis art movement of the 1970s. The brief was simple: an explosion of colors! The car of choice was a 1966 red Peugeot 404 convertible.

When I went to break down the installation, I made bouquets by using the flowers from the car to cap off the event. Each bouquet was offered to people passing by on the Canal Saint-Martin. It was a simple way to give the flowers a second life after the event.

THE CREATIVE PROPOSAL

For this flowered car, I wanted to use one of the patterns in the collection as my jumping-off point, taking my colors and shapes from there. I chose bright, vibrant colors: orange, red, blue, purple, pink, green, and yellow.

Each flower evoked the geometric shapes of the collection's print:

- round: sunflower, Aztec marigold, agapanthus, allium, zinnia
- line: delphinium, snapdragon
- semicircle: celosia
- triangle: lily petals, anthurium

SET FOR THE "FLOWER REMEDY" COLLECTION PHOTO SHOOT

Case Studies

PATTERNS FROM THE "PARIS TO MEMPHIS" COLLECTION AND PROPOSED COLOR PALETTE

SKETCH OF THE CAR

COMPLETION

Purchasing Flowers

Since this project was set up in Paris, I sourced the flowers from the Rungis flower market. I tried to purchase from as many French growers as possible. I purchased a large portion of the flowers from Karine Venet, who sells flowers at her stall from several growers from the South of France as well as flowers from the Paris region. I also went to Fleurs du Moulin to buy Aztec marigolds, delphiniums, campanula, and zinnias. I purchased privet greenery from Earl Vandendaele.

Arrangement Technique

We had very little time to install the flowers into the car. The rental company was scheduled to park it at 9 a.m. in front of the boutique, and then, at 11 a.m. sharp, we had to be ready for the opening. We thus had to be organized so we could be fast and efficient! On the basis of the dimensions of the car that the rental company sent, I determined what surface area we would flower. To cover the passenger seats and trunk quickly, we decided to use containers of flowers we had previously arranged. For the wheels on the ground, we had to use a biodegradable floral foam, so we'd be able to stick the stems into something. While we could have also used this foam in the passenger seats, I preferred to avoid it: given the size of the space to be filled, it would have meant generating too large a volume of waste, even though it was biodegradable.

Our action plan for the event was as follows.

Before the event

- Two days before the installation, I went to Rungis to buy flowers. Once I was back in the studio, we cleaned them and placed them in water to allow them time to open up.

- The night before the installation, we prepared the buckets of flowers, placing them on a table that was the same size as the passenger seats of the car. This allowed us to really understand the proportions. We also flowered the floral foam pieces we would place on the ground by the wheels.

Day of:

Step 1 • On the day of the event, we first leveled off the inside of the car, filling in the openings between the seats with cardboard. This was used to create a flat surface where the buckets could be placed.

Step 2 • We covered all the passenger seats with a plastic tarp to protect the surfaces.

Step 3 • We carefully arranged the buckets of flowers side by side inside the passenger seats, and placed the floral foam in front of the car.

Step 4 • To finish, we did some touch-ups here and there, and placed the most delicate flowers last.

Step 5 • After the event, we broke down the installation and made bouquets with the flowers.

Time for Completion and Resources

The project could be broken down into the following increments:

- two hours for the sketches and discussions before the project, approximately one month prior to the event—one person
- three hours to buy flowers in Rungis—one person
- four hours to clean plants—two people
- three hours to put flowers into containers and foam before the arrival of the car—one person
- three hours to install containers into the car and finish off the installation—three people
- three hours to take down the installation and make and distribute bouquets—three people

Approximately seven hundred stems were used for this event.

Case Studies

Marie and Alex's Wedding with Atelier Jeanne Pons

THE CLIENT

I met Sophie from Atelier Jeanne Pons when I moved to Annecy (to find her on the web, go to www.atelierjeannepons.com, @atelierjeannepons). Since that time, we have collaborated regularly on event projects. Sophie wears the dual hats of event designer and event planner. As an event designer, she designs bespoke settings for her clients. As an expert who is passionate about decor, she creates ambiance and dramatically transforms locations. As an event planner, she takes care of everything pertaining to event logistics. She directs the entire project: she scouts out a location, maintains the budget, coordinates with different providers, and manages contingencies, ensuring that her clients have nothing to worry about. Sophie works in the Annecy region and throughout France, as well as internationally.

Beyond her very beautiful creative sensibility and style, she has always demonstrated rigorous organizational skills while fostering a wonderful spirit of teamwork and conviviality among all the providers of the events she organizes. It is incidentally this art of uniting people around beautiful, generous tables that forms the heart and soul of Atelier Jeanne Pons, and it can be felt even at the professional-relations level.

Adaptability at the Heart of the Profession

I collaborate with numerous event planners and designers on event projects. Each and every one of them has their own practices and ways of working. As a provider, I have to be able to adapt and meet their expectations.

THE CLIENT BRIEF

Sophie offered me a chance to do the floral decor at Marie and Alex's wedding in July 2022. The ceremony and reception would be held at the Chateau de Duingt, an incredibly charming location along the shores of Lake Annecy. I was thrilled to have the chance to work there. The couple wanted a marriage with a bucolic feel, with everything taking place outside in the magnificent chateau gardens. For the decor and furniture, Sophie had carefully hunted down items that had an old-fashioned feel to them. There were vintage sofas upholstered in velvet, oriental rugs, demijohns, wooden crates, solid-wood door frames, and antique mismatched tableware. To punch up this assortment of items, we also planned to incorporate huge disco balls into the decor of the civil ceremony. For the flowers, the goal was to deliver a nice range of colors in arrangements with a very natural look to them. We were to provide flowers for the ceremony, cocktail hour, and dinner, as well as for the bridal party.

THE CREATIVE PROPOSAL

For this outdoor wedding, I really wanted to emphasize the bucolic feel of the location. For the area where the civil ceremony would take place, I therefore suggested placing flowers around the bride's and groom's chairs, so it would look as if they were seated in the middle of a flowering meadow. Other small "patches of grass" would likewise be installed around the lectern and in the center aisle. For the cocktail hour, I planned to put in ground gardens at various locations: on the floor of the music pavilion, and under the wooden frame used to hang the seating cards. Additionally, I planned to add some small bouquets in the lounge areas. For the meal, we decided on six flower clouds that would hang above the tables, and a table runner made from a row of small bouquets in vintage flasks, along with the two Emmanuelle armchairs for the bride and groom, each adorned with flowers and greenery. The bride's bouquet, along with boutonnieres for the groom and ushers, would complete the range of flowered elements.

Since the arrangements had to look very natural, I wanted to use a lot of foliage and grasses, along with numerous florets and wildflowers.

BREAKDOWN OF TECHNIQUES USED

Purchasing Flowers

To my great pleasure, we have begun to see flower farms take root in the Savoie and Haute-Savoie for several years now! For this project, which had a particularly countrified feel to it, I really wanted to work with at least some local flowers. I collaborated with four suppliers.

- Virginie from the Les Ombelles flower farm near Lake Geneva was able to provide me with mignonette, linaria, chamomile, cornflower, basil, oregano, cosmos, water pennywort, marigolds, branches of mint, shiso, meadowsweet, branches of sage, medium-sized stems of larkspur, dahlias, and dill.

- I selected dahlias, bee balm, zinnias, celosia, snapdragons, ageratum, verbena hastata, 'Velvet Curtains' amaranth, rudbeckia, gomphrena, and Aztec marigolds from Victor Joyeux, who grows flowers near Aix-les-Bains.

Case Studies

PROPOSED COLOR PALETTE

SKETCHES OF DIFFERENT FLORAL PIECES

- I was thrilled when Rémi from Demain au Jardin, a truck farm in Cruseilles, offered me magnificent purple and white leek flowers.
- I purchased the remaining flowers I had selected from my wholesaler: asters, sanguisorba, liatris, bells of Ireland, centaurea, panicum, white ammobium, nigella, statice, and black currant leaves.

Arrangement Techniques

For this project, we used five types of arrangement techniques: ground gardens (as seen on page 106); flower clouds (as seen on page 111), which were also used to decorate the Emmanuelle armchairs the bride and groom sat in during the meal; the bride's bouquet, which had a chicken wire base (as seen on page 94); the groom's and ushers' boutonnieres; as well as bouquets of various sizes which were placed in vases. Approximately 1,500 stems were used. We had a team of five people and we split up on the day of the event to cover the various locations to be flowered.

The biggest challenge for this event was logistics. The area we were flowering was pretty far from the unloading zone, and at the end of an uphill path. It was impossible to use a dolly, so all the flowers and other materials had to be carried by hand some 984 feet (300 meters). To top it all off, it was mid-July and incredibly hot, and I was starting my eighth month of pregnancy!

The bride's and groom's chairs for the civil ceremony were the hardest pieces to pull off, and that's why I lingered over them the longest. I had to do the entire arrangement on the day of the event, since it was impossible to begin assembly in the studio and then move the numerous components. Accordingly, we did the installation in four stages.

Step 1 • Installation of the chairs on-site.

Step 2 • Placement of various containers around the chairs. We put the containers earmarked for the tallest, and thus heaviest flowers behind the chairs, and the buckets reserved for the shortest flowers in front of them.

Step 3 • Placement of the disco balls. It's important to put in this kind of decorative element before you start placing flowers. This allows them to be fully integrated into the decor and avoids giving the impression that they were just randomly stuck there.

A GLIMPSE OF THE FLOWER CLOUDS
AND TABLE RUNNER

GROUND GARDEN BENEATH THE SEATING CARDS

Step 4 • Placement of flowers. For this kind of bold piece, we started by placing the foliage and filler flowers, to create volume and form the general shape of the arrangement. We then placed the higher-value flowers and florets.

Time to Completion and Resources

The time needed to complete the entire project could be broken down as follows:

- eight hours to create the mood board, estimate, and sketch, six months prior to the event—one person
- four hours to buy flowers for the various arrangements (choice of varieties, receipt of flowers from the wholesaler at the studio, travel to the various flower farms)—two people
- four hours to clean and display the flowers and greenery—two people
- four hours to prepare all of the containers and structures at the studio—two people
- three hours to place flowers in containers and structures at the studio—three people
- five hours to install and complete all arrangements on site—five people
- two hours to take down the installation the next day—three people
- four hours to clean the studio, wash containers, sort waste—two people

CONCLUSION

Over the course of this book, I provided a broad overview of the skills and knowledge I've gained since embarking on my adventure in flowers. It was an introspective exercise as exciting as it was dizzying. The book is a first look back, five years after my career change and two years after forming my company. Please know that I am very touched it has made it into your hands.

Now that you have this book, I often wonder what will become of it—will it live on your bookshelf, or on the floor in your studio? I hope with all my heart that sharing my experiences with you will somehow allow you to take the leap on some personal plan you have brewing, or will help you in some great project already underway. How I work has really changed over the years and will undoubtedly continue to evolve with my future encounters and experiences.

What I do know, at this precise moment as I conclude this book, is that transmitting my passion is one way I want to keep growing, in addition to my activities as a floral designer. It is so exhilarating to see an entire community of nature lovers coming together in support of the same values! I wish you all an explosion of colors and hope I can meet you soon and discover your own flowered stylings.

RESOURCES

BOOKS

Blooms: Contemporary Floral Design, Phaidon editors. New York: Phaidon Press, 2019.

The Book of Flowers, Pierre-Joseph Redouté. New York: Taschen, 2018.

Cultivated: The Elements of Floral Style, Christin Geall. Princeton: Princeton Architectural Press, 2020.

A Guide to Floral Mechanics, Sarah Diligent and William Mazuch. Hampshire, UK: Diligent & Mazuch, 2020.

Rosa, Simone Gooch. Melbourne: Perimeter Editions, 2021.

Styling Nature, Lewis Miller. New York: Rizzoli, 2016.

MAGAZINES

Blumenhaus Magazine

Plant Magazine

Pleasure Garden Magazine

Rakesprogress Magazine

PODCASTS

The Flower Podcast, Scott Shepherd

Girl Flower Podcast, Victoria Vaught and Jessica Naish

Let's Grow Girls, Nicole Laird and Sarah Hulyer

Mornings with Mayesh, Mayesh Wholesale

The Rebel Florist in Conversation, Kerry Ashby

Slow Flower Podcast, Debra Prinzing

Wedding Florist Social, Vicky Laffey

ORGANIZATIONS

Association of Specialty Cut Flower Growers (ASCFG)
  www.ascfg.org
  The ASCFG maintains LocalFlowers.org, a searchable database of members throughout North America, the UK, and Europe.

Certified American Grown (CAG)
  www.americangrownflowers.org

Flowers Canada Growers
  www.flowerscanadagrowers.com
  Also produces theflowerdirectory.com.

Society of American Florists
  www.safnow.org

United States Department of Agriculture
  The USDA's national statistics on the floriculture industry: www.nass.usda.gov/Surveys/Guide_to_NASS_Surveys/Floriculture/

Flower Industry Australia
  www.flowerindustryaustralia.com.au

British Florist Association
  www.britishfloristassociation.org

Flowers from the Farm
  www.flowersfromthefarm.co.uk
  Local flower grower network in Britain.

SUPPLIES FOR ARRANGING WITHOUT FLORAL FOAM

Agra-Wool Foam: www.agra-wool.nl/natural-floral-foam/?lang=en

Arches: www.floresieframeworks.com/solutions

Kenzan: www.niwaki.com

Wire mesh for floral foam brick:
  www.artfloral.org,
  www.instagram.com/avaeventstyling

Justine Beaussart left a corporate job to become a floral designer, and in 2021 she founded Nebbia Studio. She specializes in set designs for events and promotions, and in large-scale corporate decor. She offers workshops and online courses.

www.nebbiastudio.com | @nebbiastudio